Collins
E A P

Writing

Learn to write better academic essays

Els Van Geyte

Academic Skills Series

Collins

HarperCollins Publishers
77-85 Fulham Palace Road
Hammersmith
London W6 8JB

First edition 2013

Reprint 10 9 8 7 6 5 4 3 2 1 0

© HarperCollins Publishers 2013

ISBN 978-0-00-750710-8

www.collinselt.com

A catalogue record for this book is available from the British Library

Typeset in India by Aptara

Printed in China by South China Printing Co.

⊆ You can trust Collins COBUILD

The 4.5-billion-word Collins Corpus is the world's largest database of the English language. It is updated every month and has been at the heart of Collins COBUILD publishing for over 20 years. All definitions provided in the glossary boxes in this book have been taken from the Collins COBUILD Advanced Dictionary.

About the author

Els Van Geyte has been working at the English for International Students Unit at the University of Birmingham for over a decade, where she has been teaching English for Academic Purposes on presessional and insessional courses. She has authored two books in the Collins English for Exams Series: *Reading for IELTS* and *Get Ready for IELTS Reading*. She has also published Foreign Language courses.

Acknowledgements

I'd like to thank the many people that have helped shape this book. First of all, I am grateful to the students I have taught and learnt from over the years. I'd like to mention the following people, who let me have examples of their writing: Ali Abdalla Elhouni, Badr Alhamdan, Becky Cai, Becky McCarthy, Beyan Hariri, Guido Martinez, Ibrahim Fahad Al Dossary, Jack McCarthy, Maher Ghaneim Nawaf, Meng Yao, Netje Nada, Pham Huyen, Srwsht M. Amin, and Zhiyang Jiang. I would also like to say thank you to Josie Underhill and Susy Ridout who arranged for me to have some of the essays.

Thank you also to everyone at HarperCollins for their support, and to Daniel Rolph, Verity Cole and Alison Silver.

I am also grateful to the many people who have written books, articles and hand-outs about academic English that have helped me in my career and who ultimately inspired me to do the same.

As always, my heartfelt thanks to John and Becky McCarthy, and everyone else who has been there for me throughout my own writing process.

Contents

Contents

Introduction

Collins Academic Skills Series: Writing will build on your existing writing skills to enable you to produce successful academic essays.

Designed to be used on a self-study basis to support English for Academic Purposes or study skills courses, it is intended for students on pre-sessional or Foundation courses as well as for first year undergraduate students.

The book has eleven chapters which focus on helping you understand what is expected of you at university. It will help you with research, planning, organization, grammar, paraphrasing and much more. It will make you think about:

- the writing purpose (Chapter 1)
- the expectations of the academic reader (Chapters 2 and 4)
- content and research (Chapters 3 and 6)
- academic principles (Chapters 4, 5, 8 and 9)
- language points (Chapters 3, 5, 7 and 10)
- the writing process from start to finish (Chapter 11)

At the back of the book you will find:

- example essays: a short essay and a complete university essay, with comments on their strengths, weaknesses and differences
- advice on how to respond to marking criteria and assignment feedback
- a glossary of key terms
- a comprehensive answer key.

Chapter structure

Each chapter includes:

- Aims – These set out the skills covered in the chapter.
- A self-evaluation quiz – By doing this you are able to identify what you already know on the subject of the chapter and what you need to learn.
- Information on academic expectations and guidelines on how to develop academic skills – These sections will help you understand university practices and expectations so you know what is required.
- Practical exercises – These help you develop the skills to succeed at university. You can check your answers at the back of the book.
- Tips – Key points are highlighted for easy reference and provide useful revision summaries for the busy student.
- Glossary – Difficult words are glossed in boxes next to where the text appears in the chapter. There is also a comprehensive glossary at the back of the book.
- Remember section – This is a summary of key points for revision and easy reference.

Authentic academic texts

The book uses excerpts from academic essays, written by students who study a variety of subjects, so that you can apply what you learn to your own academic context.

Glossary boxes ⒠ POWERED BY COBUILD

Where we feel that a word or phrase is difficult to understand, we have glossed this word or phrase. All definitions provided in the glossary boxes have been taken from the *Collins COBUILD Advanced Dictionary*. At the end of the book there is a full alphabetical list of the most difficult words from the book for your reference.

Using *Writing*

You can either work through the chapters from Chapter 1 to Chapter 11 or you can choose the chapters and topics that are most useful to you. The Contents page will help in your selection.

Study tips

- Each chapter will probably take between three and four hours. Take regular breaks and do not try to study for too long. Thirty to sixty minutes is a sensible study period.
- Regular study is better than occasional intensive study.
- Read the chapter through first to get an overview without doing any exercises. This will help you see what you want to focus on.
- Try the exercises before checking the Answer key. Be an active learner.
- When writing your own essays, refer back to the appropriate sections and exercises in the book. If possible, ask a more experienced writer to give you feedback on your essay drafts.
- All university departments are different. Use the information in the book as a guide to investigating your own university department.
- Read carefully any information you receive from your department about what and how to write.
- Don't think of an essay as a finished product, but as a learning process. It is an opportunity to show that you can find out information about a subject, develop your own ideas about it, organize your thoughts and communicate your understanding to others. Don't rush this process, but find out what works best for you. Adapt the suggestions in this book to suit your learning style and context.
- With practice, writing will become easier, and your confidence will grow so that you can show your tutors your true ability and potential. We wish you every success in your academic career.

Other titles

Also available in the *Collins Academic Skills Series: Research, Lectures, Numbers, Presenting*, and *Group Work*.

1 | Essay purpose and instructions

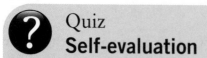
? Quiz
Self-evaluation

For each statement below, circle the word which is true for you.

1	I understand what academic writing is.	agree | disagree | not sure
2	I understand the purpose of essays.	agree | disagree | not sure
3	I know the academic meaning of instruction words in essays.	agree | disagree | not sure
4	I can find key words in essay titles to help me understand what I am expected to write.	agree | disagree | not sure
5	I can analyse the structure of an essay question to give a full answer and include the right information.	agree | disagree | not sure
6	I know who to go to at my university if I need advice about an essay.	agree | disagree | not sure

Tip ✓ When you start your degree, you will come across a lot of new words which are specific to your new environment but everybody seems to think you already understand them. Don't worry about this, but look them up as soon as possible. In this book, the words are explained in the glossary boxes and they are all in the glossary at the back.

What is academic writing?

Glossary

dissertation
(dissertations)
N-COUNT
A dissertation
is a long formal
piece of writing
on a particular
subject, especially
for a university
degree.

Academic writing is writing which is done by scholars (students or academics) for other scholars to read. It can take many forms: journal articles, textbooks, dissertations, group project reports, etc. Although students are increasingly being asked to write different types of academic text, the essay still remains the most popular type of assignment.

Essays are written by students and are likely to be read by one person only: their tutor. The essay can be set as a coursework assignment to assess a student's understanding of a module, or as an exam question.

For more information on some other types of academic writing, see Chapter 11.

The purpose of essays

Glossary

discipline
(disciplines)
N-COUNT
A discipline is a
particular area of
study, especially
a subject of
study in a college
or university.

Essays are a common form of assessment, for example in disciplines such as Business, International Relations, Law, History, Geography, Theology, Communication Studies, Education and Economics.

There are many reasons why essays are still the most popular type of assignment. One of them is that they ask students to demonstrate more than just knowledge. To demonstrate the purpose of essays, let's have a look at the difference between an ordinary question and an essay question.

> **Ordinary question:** *Why did William of Normandy win the Battle of Hastings?*
>
> **Essay question:** *William of Normandy's victory at the Battle of Hastings has often been attributed to his large and well-prepared army. However, without strategy and good fortune, he might well have lost the battle. Discuss.*

The answer to the ordinary question could be a list of items, in no particular order of importance. The essay question directs the writer more: the student has to mention the size and the preparedness of the army, describe William's strategy and the fortunate circumstances, and decide how important these elements were for the victory. In order to come to a conclusion about this, the writer has to do research. This is indicated in the language: in the first sentence 'has often been attributed to' tells the student that there are a lot of sources which she should look at to explain this point of view, and 'However' in the second sentence suggests that there is also evidence available for a contrasting opinion. The word 'Discuss' makes it clear that there are different points to be made, which should be mentioned and commented on, so that the writer can make a decision about which side she is on.

Clearly, a finished essay demonstrates more than just the knowledge students were taught about a subject. The writers will have:

- found out much more than what they were taught in lectures and seminars

- weighed up the evidence about different points of view

- developed their own point of view

- increased their knowledge and their depth of understanding

- trained their memory to remember the important facts

- undertaken activities that prepare them for their future profession.

By writing the information down in essay form, they will have:

- organized their thoughts

- practised and improved their ability to communicate in writing

- shown awareness of the reader, of academic conventions and the way others write in their discipline.

If you plan your time so that you can read up on a topic, think critically about it, follow the essay instructions, and express your view clearly in a well-organized text, you deserve a good grade.

For more information on all these aspects, see later chapters.

Analysing essay titles

Although we called the instructions in the example essay question a question, there was no question mark. The 'questions' are really titles. You will need to put the full title on your first page; don't be tempted to summarize the question and write your own title.

Your tutor may give you a long essay title, which needs to be broken down into smaller parts before it can be addressed. All essay questions will include instruction words, such as 'discuss'. For international students, these words can be particularly tricky. If you look them up in a dictionary, you may find a large number of meanings that do not always correspond exactly to the more specific meaning in the academic context, which is also why translations into other languages you may speak are unlikely to help.

For example, this is a dictionary definition of 'discuss':

> 1   to have a conversation about; consider by talking over; debate
> 2   to treat (a subject) in speech or writing ⟹ the first three volumes discuss basic principles

(Source: *Collins COBUILD Advanced Dictionary, 2008*)

Both definitions suggest that 'discuss' means 'talk (or write) about'. However, in an academic context 'discuss' often means something more specific: in order to discuss, you need to refer to different aspects of a topic, look at the benefits and drawbacks of different points of view, and give your own conclusion.

Exercise 1

In which of these essay questions does 'discuss' mean 'write about, describe', and in which does it mean more? Put a tick in the correct column.

	= write about, describe	= give different points of view (and your opinion)
1 Parliament today is less effective than it has ever been. **Discuss.**		
2 **Discuss** the geological history and likely method of formation of the Lewisian rocks.		
3 **Discuss** the circumstances that can lead to a dramatic change in the use of technology.		
4 'Current stem cell technology is sufficiently advanced for use in medicine.' **Discuss.**		

Exercise 2

In the table below, match the instruction words in the centre column with the correct academic meanings on the left. Some of the first and/or second dictionary definitions of the instruction words on the right may help you find their academic meaning.

Academic meaning	Instruction word	Dictionary definition
a state similarities and differences and draw conclusions about them	**1** show	to make, be, or become visible or noticeable
b point out weaknesses and strong points	**2** compare	to regard something as similar, to examine in order to observe similarities or differences
c demonstrate with supporting evidence	**3** justify	to prove to be just, valid or reasonable
d decide on the value or importance of a topic by giving reasons or evidence	**4** consider	to think carefully about a problem or decision
e give information but without going into details	**5** criticize	to judge (something) with disapproval, to evaluate (study) or analyse (something)
f give support for an argument	**6** assess	to judge the worth, importance, etc. of, to evaluate
g briefly and clearly describe the main points	**7** indicate	to point out or show
h give your views about a topic	**8** analyse	to break down into components or essential features, to examine in detail in order to discover meaning, essential features
i give detailed reasons or say why something is the case	**9** outline	to give the main features or general idea
j break down a topic into its different aspects and look at how they relate	**10** explain	to make (something) comprehensible, to justify by giving reasons for one's actions or words

Tip ✓ Read academic texts in your own discipline to become more aware of the conventions. For example, the instruction word 'sketch' can have completely different meanings dependent on the context. To an engineer it can mean 'draw', to a theologian it is more likely to mean 'give a brief description'.

Analysing key words and structure of essay titles

Glossary

irrelevant ADJ
If you describe
something
such as a fact
or remark as
irrelevant, you
mean that it is
not connected
with what you
are discussing or
dealing with.

Underlining or highlighting key words is a good technique which you are probably familiar with. The following is an example of an IELTS-type essay question where the most important words have been highlighted (you may find a similar question in the TOEFL test):

> *Learning to manage money is one of the key aspects of adult life.*
>
> *How in your view can individuals best learn to manage their money?*

(Source: Collins, *Writing for IELTS*, 2011)

There is usually more information in the question than you think: it can direct you both in terms of structure and content. Even a single word in the question can give you a useful clue about what you are expected to write in your essay. For example, look at the following essay title:

> *Does the media always misrepresent minority groups?*

This question tells you that the media does misrepresent minority groups, but you will still have to briefly explain this in your essay, with examples. The question is whether this is <u>always</u> the case, i.e. whether there are examples you can give where the media represents minority groups correctly. You will also have to try and explain why this is or is not the case.

When the essay question is very long however, you should also analyse the structure of the question to make sure you give a full answer without including irrelevant information.

You could follow these steps:

a   Look for the topic.

b   Use your knowledge of language to find all areas and make a note of the instruction words.

c   Use your knowledge of language to decide what should be included in your answer and what should be excluded.

Let's apply this to the following question.

> *Discuss the factors that give rise to parallel trade and evaluate how much of a problem this is for international marketers. Give examples of what a firm can do to minimize the problem.*

a   The topic is 'parallel trade'.

b   There are two sentences. The first sentence has two parts: 'Discuss the factors ... **AND** evaluate ...' . The second sentence asks you to 'give examples'. In total there are three parts.

c

Part	Instruction	What I should do
1	Discuss the factors that give rise to parallel trade.	■ define parallel trade ■ state and describe the different causes of (what 'gives rise to') parallel trade
2	Evaluate how much of a problem this is for international marketers.	■ introduce international marketing (what it is) ■ answer the questions: Is parallel trade a problem for international marketing? How much (= in which ways)? How important is this problem and why? ('evaluate' refers to importance and reasons)
3	Give examples of what a firm can do to minimize the problem.	■ answer the question: what can be done to reduce the problem of parallel trade? ■ give examples of actions that firms have taken (with positive results) or give suggestions about what they could do and say why this would work

Note that your knowledge of language helps you understand the question: 'this' refers to 'parallel trade', and 'a' in the second sentence tells you that you do not have to give examples of one specific firm, as 'a' here means 'any'.

The word 'and' is very important. Normally it means that you will need to look at two areas separately. Occasionally you could look at both areas at the same time.

Exercise 3

Analyse the following essay question using steps a, b and c. Label your answers a, b and c, writing step c in a table as shown above.

> *What are the most important key urban planning theories of the post-war period? Outline in summary their key characteristics. With reference to one of these theories, explain how they help us understand the nature of planning practice.*

Tip ✓ Increase your knowledge of language: get into the habit of observing the way academic language is used by others, and think about the meaning of words and phrases in their context.

The next exercise shows you how, by comparing phrases in different contexts, you can work out the meaning.

Exercise 4

Look at the example essay titles and work out the meaning of the highlighted word or phrase. Choose the correct multiple-choice option.

1

Why, when Britain has one of the richest economies, does homelessness still occur?

'when' here means:

A at a certain time

B at the same time

C despite the fact that

D only if

2

How is local government financed at present and how, if at all, should that financial system be reformed? Discuss.

'if at all' suggests:

A we need to take everything into consideration

B or perhaps this is not the case

C if not

D in your opinion

There are support structures in place at university. You will probably be given the name of a personal tutor, who you can see for advice. Moreover, it is unlikely that you will be given very difficult titles to start with – the first essays will probably require a relatively easy content and structure in comparison to the ones you have to write later in the academic year. You are likely to get a number of titles to choose from, and the ones in the first semester may ask you to 'describe', or 'explain', before you are asked later on to carry out more difficult tasks, such as 'analyse' or 'evaluate'. The required essay length will probably also be relatively short to start with.

Remember that it is perfectly acceptable to ask the tutor who set the question if you have understood it correctly. You will, however, need to show that you have put effort into interpreting the question.

Exercise 5

Look at the notes made by a student about an essay question. Put ✓ if you think he is right about it, ✗ if you disagree, and '?' if you think the student might have misunderstood something. Use a dictionary to help you.

> *An appreciation of politics is essential to understand the opportunities for and limitations on development.*
>
> *Analyse this statement with reference to a selected country and by reflecting on development theory and thinkers.*

This is my understanding. The question asks me to:	
1 Give an idea of how development and politics are related. (in general, probably in the introduction)	
2 State what opportunities for development come from politics. (reference to my selected country, i.e. China, with the supporting development theory and/or thinkers)	
3 State what constraints for development come from politics. (reference to my selected country, i.e. China, with the supporting development theory and/or thinkers)	
'appreciation of politics': I think I should look at the importance of politics in order to relate it to the development. (somehow I wonder if there is any further meaning than that or how I can incorporate the appreciation of politics into my answers)	
The question says theory and thinker. For the thinker part: in my understanding, a thinker is a person that states his/her idea about certain topics. So in this case, I can use his/her opinion and thought to support my point. It does not have to be theory related.	

Remember

✓ Break down the essay question to identify its exact meaning.

✓ To analyse a question you need to look in detail and use your knowledge of English to understand the clues about what is expected.

✓ Don't be afraid to ask for help with understanding the question.

✓ You need to demonstrate the ability to evaluate different points of view and demonstrate research skills.

✓ You need to show awareness of the reader, of academic conventions and the way others in the discipline write.

2 | Reader expectation and essay structure

? Quiz
Self-evaluation

For each statement below, circle the word which is true for you.

1	I know how to write an outline for an essay based on an analysis of the essay title.	agree | disagree | not sure
2	I know what I am normally expected to include in the introduction to an essay.	agree | disagree | not sure
3	I always write my introduction first.	agree | disagree | not sure
4	I know what to include in the conclusion of an essay.	agree | disagree | not sure
5	I know how to use signposting and cohesion to guide the reader through my essay.	agree | disagree | not sure
6	I know what the parts of a paragraph usually are.	agree | disagree | not sure

Making your essay more readable

Your assessor is mainly concerned with the content of your essay. This partly depends on your research skills but also on your ability to get your points across.

You can make your essay easy to read in a number of ways, e.g. by using a clear structure and by guiding the reader through the text.

Essay structure

Glossary

outline (outlines)
N-VAR
An outline
is a general
explanation or
description of
something.

principle
(principles)
N-COUNT
The principles
of a particular
theory or
philosophy are
its basic rules or
laws.

When you wrote shorter essays, you learnt that the basic structure is: introduction / main body / conclusion, and that each separate idea needs a new paragraph. When you are writing a longer essay, the main principles are the same, but there are some differences.

The same three-part structure applies to any essay. In a longer essay, the introduction and conclusion will be more developed, but the biggest change will be in the main body, where there will be much more space to develop ideas. Although each new idea will still require a new paragraph, these separate ideas are likely to need more than one paragraph each to be fully developed. Before you do your research, you won't know how many paragraphs you will be writing, but you are able to do an outline of the structure of the whole essay from the start.

The method we used in Chapter 1 can be used here to help with structure too. Look back at the example essay question about parallel trade and the three-step analysis of this question in the section *Analysing key words and structure of essay titles*.

This breakdown will lead to your outline, which can function as a plan for your writing as well as a starting point for your research.

Here, it would look like this:

Introduction	background about parallel trade, including definition
Main body	Paragraph 1 ■ a description of each of the causes of parallel trade Paragraph 2 ■ the aims of international marketers / an explanation of the different problems that parallel trade causes them Paragraph 3 ■ the importance of these problems, with reasons Paragraph 4 ■ possible solutions with examples
Conclusion	comments about how big the problem of parallel trade is for international marketers and if it can be successfully minimized

Exercise 1

Write an outline for the essay title below, from Chapter 1 Exercise 3. Before you start the outline, look at the Answer key for Chapter 1 for the three-step analysis of the essay title.

> *What are the most important key urban planning theories of the post-war period? Outline in summary their key characteristics. With reference to one of these theories, explain how they help us understand the nature of planning practice.*

The last thing you want to do is confuse your reader, so it is important to structure your work in the order that they would expect to find it.

The introduction

In an introduction you would normally:

1   give a description or explanation of the situation or problem (more general)

2   say why this situation or problem (or a more specific aspect of it) is important

3   say what your aim is, what your position on the situation or problem is, and what the organization of your essay will be.

The main function of the introduction is to show your reader you have understood the question and to indicate that you will be discussing it fully. You do not have to go into detail yet.

It is difficult to say how long an introduction should be, but as you won't be starting to discuss anything in any detail yet, it won't be long. It is likely to be less than 10 per cent of the word count.

Until you have finished your research, you might not be sure exactly what the structure of your essay will be, so it is a good idea to write your introduction last.

Exercise 2

Look at these two introductions of 1,000-word essays. Look at the three things you would normally include in an introduction above and then think about how you would improve the introductions.

> *'It would be better not to let pupils use calculators at all in their maths lessons.' Discuss.*

Introduction A

It may be a good idea not to let students use calculators in maths classes, but there are also reasons why they can be helpful. This essay will first address the role calculators play by considering their benefits, as well as possible drawbacks. Then I shall present a simple argument for the use of calculators by examining the fundamental purpose of an educational system before concluding that we should not reject the use of calculators in a learning environment.

Introduction B

Calculators are useful pieces of equipment and are very popular in mathematical learning. However, some of their functions have raised concerns with maths teachers about the harmful effects on the students' ability to improve their learning. This is why the idea of forbidding the use of calculators is being discussed. I think this opinion is too extreme and limited.

The conclusion

Your conclusion will normally consist of:

1 a summary of the main ideas (related to the importance to the topic)

2 a summary of your evidence (with your evaluation of it)

3 your overall conclusion / your answer to the question.

The conclusion will be more specific than the introduction, as you will already have mentioned the ideas you are commenting on. Do not add any new evidence or ideas: if you have more to say, then this should be done in the body of the text. Like your introduction, your conclusion is likely to contain no more than 10 per cent of the word count.

Exercise 3

Look at the ending of this 1,500-word essay and identify the three different parts of the conclusion. The first part has been identified for you.

> In conclusion, (1) new technologies have provided a remarkable breakthrough which has allowed society itself to become incredibly advanced. They have now become so highly developed that they have provoked ethical questions about their morality. One of the main reasons for this is that they can be controlling, but as we have seen, they are liberating at the same time, with cyborg (mechanical body parts) technology even being able to save people's lives. Another area of thought is related to the area of feminism: despite their large contribution to the fields of science and technology, women still have to struggle with inequality in everyday and scientific life. While new technologies have undoubtedly influenced postmodern thinking, the amount of research activity in the field in recent years suggests that the influence may also work the other way round.

The main body

The main body of the text consists of a number of paragraphs, blocks of text that develop ideas. We will look at them in more detail below in *The structure of paragraphs*.

For more information on the language used in introductions, conclusions and the main body, see Chapter 3.

Guiding your reader

The longer your piece of writing is, the more important it is that you guide your reader through it. You can do this by telling them about the structure (signposting), by using language that shows that the different aspects of your writing relate to each other (cohesion) and by distinguishing clearly between paragraphs (paragraphing).

Glossary

cohesion
N-UNCOUNT
If you write with cohesion, you use language that shows that the different aspects of your writing relate to each other, fit together well, and form a united whole.

distinguish
(distinguishes, distinguishing, distinguished)
VERB
If you distinguish one thing from another or distinguish between two things, you show, see, or understand how they are different.

guild (guilds)
N-COUNT
A guild is an organization of people who do the same job or activity.

Let's have a look at how a student did this in a short piece of writing. (He has made several mistakes, which are discussed below.)

This essay will look at how young people can be encouraged to vote in two main ways.

Firstly, the government should devise campaigns to inform them and increase their awareness of the importance of voting.

To start with, these campaigns should be as informal as possible and use electronic media such as blogs, websites or any other means that are accessible to that generation. Later on, the medium could also include newspapers and posters.

In addition, the contents of the campaigns should include the fact that voting is the right of every citizen, and state the benefits of voting such as the ability to choose the right representative for a particular area. It is also important to inform the young citizens that it is easy for them to vote.

Finally, after all the campaigns are done through the many information channels, the government may also promote voting by educating people in colleges, student guilds and other student organizations.

In conclusion, by taking these approaches, hopefully more young people will vote.

The student has indicated in the first sentence that there are two approaches he will discuss (but he could have made it clearer that these are media campaigns and educational programmes). He uses linking words to indicate the structure of his discussion: 'Firstly' and 'Finally' introduce the two areas he will discuss. He also uses other linking words.

Many students have been taught that linking words are very important, but some use these types of words too often. This is the case in this example. 'In addition' could be crossed out without it affecting the meaning: 'the contents of the campaigns' gives more information about a topic that was already raised, which is a natural thing to do, so the reader does not need to be told there is a link. It is also a bad choice of linker: it does not introduce an additional idea, but a more specific one. Here the linking words are all used at the beginning of a paragraph, making the text sound very repetitive (if you read it out loud, you will notice the pattern repeating). To sum up, linking words can be helpful to guide the reader, but you should only use them if they are necessary; make sure you use an appropriate one, and vary their place in the sentence.

Some of the words refer to other words in the text:

- the pronouns 'them' and their' in the second sentence refer to 'young people' in the first sentence

- 'these campaigns' in the third sentence refers back to the campaigns mentioned in the second sentence, and 'that generation' refers back to 'young people'

- the article 'the' in 'the medium', 'the campaigns' and 'the young citizens' indicates that these ideas have already been mentioned.

We can group some of the words mentioned, to show how a number of ideas are developed throughout the text. There are words related to the areas of:

- youth: young people, that generation, young citizens

- education: campaigns, inform, awareness, contents, fact, information channels, educating, contents, colleges, student guilds, student organizations

- media: blogs, websites, medium, newspapers, posters, information channels

- voting: vote, citizen, choose, representative

Visually, a space has been left between each paragraph. This is the right thing to do, although indents are also acceptable. In this short piece of writing, there was no need to have so many paragraphs. For example, the one that begins with 'To start with' develops the idea from the previous paragraph and should have been part of that one.

Exercise 4

Cross out the unnecessary and/or incorrect linking words in the paragraph (taken from an IELTS-type essay). Do not make any other changes.

It is widely believed that the internet is making our lives easier than they were in the past. Furthermore, the internet is used as a consultation method for solving many problems. On the one hand, many people use the internet for consulting others who are in a different location, for example, teachers, physicians and community researchers. Moreover, there are social networking sites such as Facebook to communicate with old friends, and so you can get together with them and other people you have not seen in a long time. The internet has also led to an increase in opportunities for face-to-face communication and people can talk with each other at any time and anywhere. At last, people with disabilities can use the internet to help overcome obstacles so that they have better access to education and other services.

Exercise 5

Underline the pronouns in this text and think about how they are used to connect the ideas in the text.

> Internet users can get information any time they need it via their internet connection. When the internet was first introduced, its feature was to share information. As time has gone by, more functions and tools have been added. These include blogs, which allow users to share their comments and opinions, and social networks, which enable people to pass on messages quickly.

The structure of paragraphs

Glossary

obstacle
(obstacles)
N-COUNT
You can refer to anything that makes it difficult for you to do something as an obstacle.

A paragraph normally has three parts:

1   a sentence that introduces the topic (and possibly links it to the previous paragraph)

2   a number of sentences that develop the topic (with analysis, evidence or detail)

3   a sentence that concludes the topic (or links it to the next topic/ paragraph).

Have a look at some examples, where the sections have been numbered (1), (2) and (3).

> *(1) Corruption is the most important point to focus on, because this originates where the power is. (2) Corruption can take many forms: political, which involves corruption in a country's legal system and police force, and economic, for example misuse of taxes and foreign aid money. (3) A country with a corrupt government is not able to develop.*
>
> *(1) Another obstacle facing the developing nations today is capital flight. (2) This is the rapid movement of investments out of a country. This can be for economic reasons, such as an increase in taxes. It often also happens as a result of political problems such as internal or external wars. (3) It has a negative impact on the trust that people have in their governments, and investors tend to invest in other countries.*

Tip

Tip ✓ Did you notice how common the pattern of three is? There are three parts in an essay, three parts in an introduction, three parts in a conclusion, and three parts in a paragraph. When you plan and write your essays, the three-part structure can help you order and shape your ideas.

Connecting paragraphs

Glossary

argument
(arguments)
N-VAR
An argument is
a statement or
set of statements
that you use
in order to try
to convince
people that your
opinion about
something is
correct.

measure
(measures)
N-COUNT
When someone,
usually a
government or
other authority,
takes measures
to do something,
they carry
out particular
actions in order
to achieve a
particular result.

policy (policies)
N-VAR
A policy is a set
of ideas or plans
that is used as a
basis for making
decisions,
especially in
politics,
economics, or
business.

When you start a new paragraph, you are indicating that the previous point is finished and you are starting something new. However, this new paragraph is not completely separate from the previous one, and you will have to indicate what the relationship is. For example, if you start with 'Another argument in favour of calculators is ...', then the language you have chosen clearly indicates to the reader that you are discussing a different argument ('Another') with the same purpose ('in favour').

When you use a construction like 'another argument is', what you are doing is summing up what has been said previously and naming it ('argument'). You are also announcing what you are going to be doing next ('<u>another</u> argument'), or perhaps indicating that you are going to give more specific information ('<u>This</u> argument ...').

The following are examples of words like 'argument', which are often used with the word 'this' (or 'these', when used in the plural) in this way.

> analysis, approach, concept, context, data, definition, environment, evidence, factor, function, interpretation, issue, measure, method, period, policy, principle, procedure, process, research, response, sector, structure, theory

Here is an example of how this pattern can be used. Note that some information has been left out of the paragraphs.

> The government wanted to introduce social security as part of a larger policy to improve society. [...] Another important message was that they felt that the state and the individual should work together. This meant that social security was not intended to discourage people from taking responsibility for improving their lives [...].
>
> <u>These</u> guiding <u>principles</u> [...].

Note that the first sentence of a paragraph will normally show how it fits in with the overall structure of your plan, and may indicate what will happen next.

Tip ✓ Check the logical construction of your own writing by highlighting the most important sentences in each paragraph. If you just read those, would the essay make sense? If not, make changes.

For more information on the language used to introduce, develop and connect paragraphs, see Chapter 3.

Remember

✓ Essay structure – introduction / body / conclusion. The body is likely to have a large number of well-developed and linked paragraphs.

✓ Planning – do an initial outline based on an analysis of the essay question; a more detailed one can be done after the research.

✓ Introduction – includes an explanation of the situation and its importance, as well as a statement of the aim of the essay and an indication of its structure.

✓ Conclusion – includes a summary of the main ideas, a review and evaluation of the evidence, and an answer to the question.

✓ Paragraphs have a three-part structure with their own introductory and concluding sentence(s), and analysis, evidence or detail in between; they often refer forward and backwards to other paragraphs.

✓ Readability becomes very important in long essays. The reader needs to find the right information where they expect it; they also need to be told about the structure of the essay and find cohesive text, divided into paragraphs and signposted throughout.

✓ Linking words need to be used in longer text; they need to be chosen carefully and used only where necessary.

3 | Essay content and language

Aims ✓ explain the time frame, situation and certainty
✓ define key terms and concepts
✓ indicate the importance of the topic and organization of the essay
✓ use organizational patterns and visuals
✓ understand the language of conclusions

? Quiz
Self-evaluation

For each statement below, circle the word which is true for you.

1	I think the first sentence of an essay should be very general.	agree | disagree | not sure
2	I know how to define key terms and concepts in an introduction.	agree | disagree | not sure
3	I can indicate the importance of the topic in an introduction correctly.	agree | disagree | not sure
4	I know how to introduce the aim and organization of the essay.	agree | disagree | not sure
5	I can use organizational patterns and visuals in an essay.	agree | disagree | not sure
6	I understand how to use tenses correctly in a conclusion.	agree | disagree | not sure

Content and language

In Chapter 2, we discussed how your essay question can be analysed to produce an outline that shows in which section of your essay you will discuss each part. Here we look at the content and language of introductions, the main body and conclusions.

The beginning of the essay

The essay has to introduce the topic, so must start with a relatively general comment. The trick is not to over-generalize, otherwise the comment becomes meaningless. For example, the following first sentences of an essay are too vague or general.

First sentence of essay	Comments	Possible improvement
1 Most people hold firmly to the belief that the English language is one of the most popular languages in the world.	English being 'one of the most popular languages in the world' is a fact, not a belief. The student wanted to use 'hold firmly to the belief', but this language is not right for the content. The statement also seems to be too general: it is not clear what this essay will be about.	The English language is spoken as a first or second language by millions of people, and is becoming even more popular because of its use in electronic communication.
2 Nowadays, many people spend their time watching TV or surfing the internet.	As in the previous example, this sentence says something that most people know, but it does not clearly introduce the topic of the essay. The word 'nowadays' is over-used at the beginning of essays.	In the past few decades, traditional pastimes such as reading books have become less popular than technology-based activities such as watching TV and surfing the internet.
3 The need to have a higher degree has often been debated recently.	The student says something that perhaps is not really true: has this really often been debated recently? It looks as if she wanted to use the language 'has often been debated recently', which could be said about any topic (the need to use cleaner energy, the need for more public transport, etc.). Even if it is true about the debate, the sentence is not saying much.	The recent rises in tuition fees for first and higher degrees have led to sharp drops in student numbers.

The following examples get it just right: they are not too general, nor too specific.

4 Globalization, a 21st century phenomenon, is having a great impact on countries, not just economically, but also culturally, educationally and socially.

5 Compared to the past we are living in an educated era, with more people attending universities and increasing numbers going abroad to study.

You will have noted from the comments about examples 1–3 that it is not a good idea to memorize words or phrases ('nowadays', 'has been debated') to insert your ideas into. It is better to start from your ideas and then to think about how they are best expressed. To do this, you need to think about the time frame, the situation and the certainty.

Although you are generalizing, don't be vague about the situation and when it happened.

If we analyse what the verbs describe in examples 1–5 above (looking at the improved versions in the column on the right for 1–3), we will find the present continuous tense (*is becoming, is having, are living*) in examples 1, 4 and 5, which describe ongoing processes. In examples 2 and 3 the present perfect is used, to link a past situation with the present (*have become, have led*). There is also an example of the present passive form (*is spoken*) in example 1. Notice that generalizations are unlikely to be expressed in the past tense, unless they are about historical situations.

For more information on tenses, see Chapter 5.

Notice that generalizations often use plural nouns (*people, tuition fees, student numbers*), and uncountable nouns, i.e. a noun that has no plural form (*globalization*). It would be strange to use a singular countable noun (*person, student*), unless it represents a larger category as in the example '*A student needs to be able to raise thousands of pounds a year*', where the word 'student' does not relate to a particular student, but to '*any student*'. The sentence has the same meaning as '*Students need to be able ...*'

In the original sentence in example 2, the writer states a truth, without saying what the relevance of it is for the essay. The addition of 'technology-based activities' in the improved version tells the reader why surfing the internet and watching TV are mentioned, especially as there is also a contrast with 'traditional pastimes'. This adds an element of precision, even though the sentence remains general.

Precision is also present in example 4: we know which aspects of globalization the writer is going to discuss. By mentioning the four categories, the writer also indicates the structure of the essay.

You need to indicate very clearly what is fact and what is not.

The claim in (improved) example 1 is that the English language is popular, and the evidence for this is that it is spoken as a first or second language by millions of people and that it is used in electronic communication (which makes it become even more popular).

The writer of example 1 presents a fact and evidence. In example 3, we can read about a cause and its effect. These claims are strong, as evidence is provided.

When less evidence is available, it is better to be cautious and use language that expresses your degree of certainty. This can be done through adverbs (*usually*, *often*, *undoubtedly*, *probably*, *unlikely*), adjectives (*most*, *some*, *certain*) and modal verbs (*can*, *may*, *might*).

For more information on cautious language, see Chapters 8 and 9.

Definitions

Definitions can occur in the introduction or the main part of the essay. Key concepts are most likely to be defined in the introduction.

It is normal practice to define your key terms, but it becomes especially important to include definitions if you use the words in a meaning which is different from the usual interpretation, or if you are using one meaning when there are many.

Look at the following ways to define an important concept:

synthesis	is	the process of combining objects or ideas into a complex whole
	is commonly defined as	
	is generally understood to refer to	
	can be described as	

the process of combining objects or ideas into a complex whole	is called	synthesis
	is known as	
	is referred to as	

Notice how the passive form is often used (*is defined*, *can be described*, *is called*, *is known*, *is referred to*). Typical mistakes that are made with the passive are forgetting the form of 'to be' and not using the past participle (e.g. writing *define* where it should be *defined*). Remember that passive forms have a form of 'to be' followed by the past participle of the verb.

Study the tables above. Then try to do Exercise 1 without looking back at the tables.

Exercise 1

Define the word 'comprehension' (= the act or ability to understand) in two ways: once starting the sentence with the word, and once ending the sentence with the word. Use passive forms of the verb each time.

Definitions often use relative clauses after a noun to indicate which person or which thing we are talking about, for example:

> *Notation is a method of recording music,* which is based on naming the notes by letters and also includes ways of distinguishing the value of notes in terms of duration.

The relative pronoun that is used here is 'which'. Other relative pronouns that are often used after a noun in this way are *who*, *whose* (which expresses possession), and *that*.

Exercise 2

Fill in the missing relative pronouns in the following definitions. Choose from *that*, *which*, *whose* and *who*.

1   The wings of a bird or insect are the two parts of its body _____ it uses for flying.

2   A wing of an organization, especially a political organization, is a group _____ is part of it and _____ has a particular function or particular beliefs.

3   In a theatre, the wings are the sides of the stage _____ are hidden from the audience by curtains or scenery.

4   A choir is an organized group of singers _____ usually sing in church services.

5   A long, thin container _____ you squeeze in order to force paste out is referred to as a tube.

If you are using a particular definition or interpretation, perhaps from a choice of many, you will need to use longer structures to explain this, and may need to include a justification of your choice. Some examples are:

> **Using definitions**
>
> - For the purposes of this essay, I will be using Kotler's definition of societal marketing, because of its focus on the organization's task to meet the need of the clients and to '... deliver the desired satisfactions more effectively and efficiently than competitors, in a way that preserves or enhances the consumer's and the society's well-being.'
>
> - Although many different definitions of marketing have been suggested over the years, I will be using the one by Kotler (1994), because of ... .
>
> - Throughout this essay, I will be using the word 'cognitive' to refer to the different types of intellectual behaviour.
>
> - In this essay, the term 'reliability' is used to mean ...

Indicating the importance of the topic

Superlatives can be useful to indicate that the topic is a relevant one:

(one of) **the most**	significant important	causes of ... problems of ...	is ...
(some of) **the most**		conditions for ... aspects of ...	are ...

... is	(one of) **the most**	significant important	causes of ... problems of ... conditions for ... aspects of ...

The following **adjective** and noun combinations can also be useful:

> **Adjective and noun combinations**
>
> an **important** part, a **key** role/factor, a **great/major** problem, a **central** area of, a **common** problem, an **increasing** need/concern, **heightened** awareness, **rapid** development, a **dramatic** increase, **renewed/ unprecedented** interest, a **serious** effect/impact on, **increasing** concern

You can also use the following combinations with **adverbs**:

is becoming **increasingly** important, has been **extensively** researched

Introducing the aim and the organization of the essay

You could use the following patterns:

This essay	will	examine whether ...
	attempts to	determine whether ...
The aims of this essay	are to	

This essay	examines whether ...
	determines whether ...
	argues that ...

In this essay	I argue that ...
	I will discuss ...
	it will be argued that ...

Notice how 'will' and present tenses are used (*will examine*). 'Will' is used to announce what is to come. Present forms are used (*examines*) to state a fact about the organization of the essay.

There is a choice between passive forms (*it will be argued that*) or active forms with 'I' (*I will argue that*).

When you announce the structure of the essay, the form with 'I' is common. For example:

I will first discuss the reasons why Galen originally became popular. In the second section, I will offer explanations for his enduring popularity, after which I will explain the part that was played by the church and the state.

The main body: Organizational patterns

Essays can be organized in a variety of ways. Some examples of organizational patterns are: comparing/contrasting, problem/solution, chronological, description, exemplifying, classifying, themes, definition, process, cause/effect, advantages/disadvantages, strengths/weaknesses/opportunities/threats (SWOT).

In shorter essays, it is more likely that a pattern is used throughout the whole essay. In longer essays, you are more likely to use a combination. For example, if you are writing an essay about the Cadbury Company, you could use a chronological pattern, in which you write events in the order in which they occurred. Within the different periods, you might use cause and effect, you could include extended definitions of different business models, you could recount a SWOT analysis that was carried out, etc.

Exercise 3

Match the language on the left with the functions on the right.

1 A good illustration of this is the study carried out by De Carvalho (2012).	listing/classifying
2 There are three factors that can explain why the practice has not become more widespread. Firstly, ...	giving cause/effect
3 This demonstrated that a different perspective on the problem can give rise to alternative decisions being taken.	exemplifying
4 Whereas in Western societies this is the most important factor in deciding attractiveness, in Eastern societies this is less so.	comparing/contrasting

Using visuals

In your essays, you may not always need to include visuals, but when you do they will be in the main body. You always need to introduce the visual in your text before showing it. After the visual, you need to describe the most important information contained in it. This may be done by comparing or contrasting, describing change over time, interpreting statistics, etc.

The visuals could be either tables or figures. The title (also sometimes called 'caption' or 'figure legend') of a table needs to be put **above** the table, but it needs to be put **underneath** the information for a figure. You will need to indicate the source of the table or figure. If you have designed or compiled it yourself, then you need to indicate this in the text. For example:

The following figure shows an overview of the different opinions expressed in both studies. I have put the negative ones on the left and the positive ones on the right.

The language of conclusions

Look at the following conclusion:

The institute for health improvement has identified that an open visiting policy in intensive care units is an important aspect of quality improvement. (1) The aim of this paper was to evaluate and compare the benefits and risks of open and restricted visiting policies. (2) Although the advantages and benefits of visitors for patients have been reported in various studies, the risks and disadvantages have also been discussed.

(3) It is difficult to adapt the same visiting policy across intensive care units and every situation should be assessed on an individual basis. To avoid any adverse effects of visits on staff and patients, staff should be educated on visitor needs and behaviour, and also brochures should be developed and provided which outline the visiting policies.

Notice how the student repeats the aim of the paper in sentence (1). He also says what type of evidence has been discussed in the essay in sentence (2). The overall conclusion and recommendations come at the end (3).

Have a look at the tenses used in the underlined words in the conclusion above. The aim has now been fulfilled, so is referred to in the past simple. The essay itself is not completely finished yet, so the present perfect is used: this tense provides a link between the past and the present. In conclusions that refer to concrete facts, the present tense is used. Recommendations are often made by using 'should'.

Exercise 4

Answer the following questions.

1   Fill in the correct verb forms in the following sentences, taken from conclusions.

   a   This essay (to discuss) _____ the economic factors that contributed to ...

   b   In this essay, I (argue) _____ that globalization is not a recent phenomenon.

   c   This essay (explore) _____ the causes of the conflict ...

2   What tense did you use in sentences a–c?

3   The following sentences summarize the evidence and give an indication of their importance. You need to use a different tense here. Which one and why?

   a   These findings (to suggest) _____ that ...

   b   The evidence (to seem) _____ to indicate that ...

   c   A consequence of this (to be) _____ that ...

Remember

✓   At the start of your essay, don't give any details but say something meaningful.

✓   The language you use (tenses, singular or plural, modal verbs, etc.) will depend on the situation you are describing, its time frame and the strength of your claims.

✓   Define your concepts, indicate the importance of the topic, and state the aims and organization of the essay in the introduction.

✓   Decide on the best organizational pattern for your essay and remember that most essays will use a combination of patterns.

✓   Integrate visuals into your essay by introducing them before inserting them, labelling them correctly, and explaining the most significant information in them.

✓   Use the correct tenses in conclusions to sum up what the essay discussed and comment on its importance.

4 | Formality, efficiency, modesty and clarity

Aims
- ✓ understand **formality** in register and style
- ✓ understand **efficiency** in register and style
- ✓ understand **modesty** in register and style
- ✓ understand **clarity** in register and style

Aims

? Quiz
Self-evaluation

For each statement below, circle the word which is true for you.

1	I often use words like 'big', 'good', 'a lot' in my essays.	agree | disagree | not sure
2	It is generally acceptable to use idioms and contractions in academic writing.	agree | disagree | not sure
3	I always proofread my essays to make sure I haven't repeated myself.	agree | disagree | not sure
4	I know how to use cautious and impersonal language to make my writing modest.	agree | disagree | not sure
5	It is acceptable to use words like 'thing', 'kind of', 'stuff' in academic writing.	agree | disagree | not sure
6	I feel I need to write long and complex sentences to write in an academic style.	agree | disagree | not sure

Four principles of academic writing

Glossary

genre (genres)
N-COUNT
A genre is a particular type of literature, painting, music, film, or other art form which people consider as a class because it has special characteristics.

In Chapter 2 we looked at what the person marking your work wants. One aspect of this is that you need to demonstrate that you understand the conventions of the academic genre.

In this chapter we will be looking at what all academic readers want, i.e. the type of register and style that is expected from all scholars.

We will look at four principles of academic writing: Formality, Efficiency, Modesty, and Clarity, and consider what they mean for the academic writer. For each principle, you will find examples of mistakes students have made, followed by explanations and corrections. Try to work out what the mistakes are and how you could correct them before you read on.

Formality

Glossary

formality
N-UNCOUNT
If you talk about the formality of a person's language or writing style, you mean that they are using extremely formal academic language.

Before starting university, students are already aware of the need for formal language in essays. The problem is that it can be difficult to know what is formal and what is not. You can try to think about it in this way: words that are used a lot when speaking (e.g. 'big', 'good', 'well', 'a lot'), or a technique that is used a lot in speeches (e.g. asking the audience questions) are unlikely to be used in formal writing.

> What else can we expect from the internet? The first thing which we expect and hope to have is an improvement of the services in the near future.

The student asks a question here and then answers it. This is a technique used in speeches to involve the audience. In academic writing, the writer does not address the audience. An improvement would be: 'The future of the internet will be decided by the needs of its customers. One development is therefore likely to be service improvement.' This takes out the question, the word 'hope', which is quite personal, and the need for 'we', which refers to internet customers.

Writing

Glossary

analogy
(analogies)
N-COUNT
If you make or
draw an analogy
between two
things, you show
that they are
similar in some
way.

metaphor
(metaphors)
N-VAR
A metaphor is an
imaginative way
of describing
something
by referring
to something
else which is
the same in a
particular way.
For example, if
you want to say
that someone
is very shy and
frightened of
things, you might
say that they are
a mouse.

> Secondly, we need to reduce the internet service access fees. Moreover, there are always technological developments in the pipeline.

This follows on from the previous text about the internet, so we can avoid the 'we' by saying 'Another customer requirement is a reduction in access fees.' The second sentence contains an idiom, 'in the pipeline', which means 'in the process of being completed, delivered, or produced'. Idioms are very rare in academic writing, and it is better if you don't use them. The sentence could be improved as follows:

> *'Technological advances can also be expected, as companies are always developing their systems in order to stay competitive.'*

> Analysis of annual financial reports is an art, which involves many complexities. Even when they are looking at the same natural beauty, amateur painters and great masters will have completely different interpretations. Different people might obtain different conclusions when reading the same report.

This student is using an analogy: financial analysis is compared to an art form with many complexities. It is not wrong to use an analogy, as it involves comparison, which is an academic skill. However, analogy and metaphor can be quite poetic in nature, in which case they are not academic. The student is going too far in the second sentence. An improvement would be: 'The analysis of financial reports can be said to have more in common with art than with science, as it relies on interpretation and not just facts. This is why different analysts may reach different conclusions.'

> Then, there is another problem: different parties' interests often correspond with the financial performance of the company.

'Then' is used here to list items ('First, ... Second, ... Then, ...'). This is often done in presentations, but in writing it sounds too informal. The sentence can be improved as follows: 'Another problem is that different parties' interests ...'.

> In order to find out more information about the statement, the reader can break it down into its different aspects.

Glossary

phrasal verb
(phrasal verbs)
N-COUNT
A phrasal verb
is a combination
of a verb and
an adverb or
preposition, for
example 'shut
up' or 'look
after', which
together have
a particular
meaning.

Notice how one-word verbs sound more formal than phrasal verbs: 'In order to <u>investigate</u> further, the reader can <u>analyse</u> the different aspects of the statement.'

> In companies with alternative working environments there seems to be a lot more respect for the management.

'A lot' is so common in speech that it is best avoided in academic writing. It can simply be replaced with 'much' in front of an uncountable word (like 'respect' in this sentence), or 'many' if it is countable (e.g. 'many people').

> However, every enterprise cannot develop without the support of society and the natural resources of the environment.

There is a grammatical mistake here: you wouldn't say 'every X cannot'. One way of correcting this is saying 'an enterprise cannot ...'. This can be made to sound more formal by using 'no' instead of 'not': '... no enterprise can ...'.

> There are not many recruitment managers who would actually use social networking sites to gather information about potential employees.

In a similar way to the previous example, we can replace 'not' to make the sentence more formal: 'Few recruitment managers would ...'. Where 'not ... much' is used in an essay, it can be replaced with 'little'.

> Firstly, the leader should implement systems which enable the staff to tackle their problems together.

An improvement would be: '... enable the staff to solve their problems together'. 'Tackle' is often used in the context of sport, and is quite an informal word. There is a good alternative available, so it is better to use that here.

> Patients can't always judge accurately what is expected of them.

Using abbreviated forms of verbs (*can't*, *shouldn't*, *won't*, etc., instead of *cannot*, *should not* and *will not*) is fine in informal writing such as emails, but contractions are not acceptable in academic writing.

Tip

Tip ✓ It is easy to check for contractions when you are proofreading: you can do a software search for the apostrophe (') and, if it is part of a contraction, you can replace it easily.

Formality is not about writing difficult words and constructions. If you try to over-complicate your language, it may give the impression you are not being respectful of the reader. Instead, when you are explaining something in your text, start off simply, then rephrase parts to make the writing more formal.

Exercise 1

Is the style in this book formal or informal? Find examples to illustrate your answer. Why do you think this style has been chosen?

Efficiency

Glossary

efficiency
N-UNCOUNT
Efficiency is the quality of being able to do a task successfully, without repetition or wasting time or energy.

Efficient writing fulfils its purpose without saying too much. You should use the minimum amount of language that is required, and not repeat yourself. When you were writing shorter essays for exams, you might have been worried about writing enough words in a small amount of time, which may have led to repetition. Avoid this by careful proofreading.

> To compare these two theories, several examples of similar content can be pointed out between these two theories.

There was no need to repeat 'theories'. An improvement would be: 'When comparing these two theories, it becomes clear that there are many similarities.'

Tip

Tip ✓ Although you are not expected to know every word, the words that relate to the essay topic will have featured in the materials you read during your research. Make a note of useful vocabulary as you read.

If you look carefully at academic writing, you will notice that many noun phrases are used. Here is an example:

> '*In a **study**, the **effect** of **weight loss** without **salt restriction** on the **reduction** of **blood pressure** in overweight **patients** was examined*.'

Nearly half of the words in that sentence are nouns. Using nouns is efficient: you use less space if you are talking about processes (salt reduction) without describing the action (they have reduced the salt).

Modesty

Exercise 2

Make these sentences more academic by using nouns instead of verbs where possible. Underline the verbs first, then transform some of them into nouns, e.g.:

The country <u>would benefit</u> if corporations <u>increase</u> the amount they <u>produce</u>.

An increase in corporate productivity would benefit the country.

1   The company will have to train their staff better so that they can be more efficient.

2   In this case, there is a difference between cultures so they need to communicate by using varied strategies.

3   If they adopt this strategy, they may reduce the costs.

4   If they create such a unit, they may have better access to marketing information.

Glossary

modesty
N-UNCOUNT
If you write with modesty, you use impersonal and cautious language in your writing.

In academic writing you need to be respectful of the ideas of others. In your essays it is very unlikely that you would say something like 'These researchers were completely wrong.' Instead you might say 'More recent research has shown that this is not the case.' You are supposed to look at different angles and say whether you agree or disagree, but you always need to remain modest about your opinion. Look at some examples on the next page:

> Trait theory is the best leadership theory.

Glossary

cite (cites, citing, cited) VERB
If you cite something, you quote it or mention it, especially as an example or proof of what you are saying.

This statement is too strong: even if the student can explain why this theory is useful in comparison to other theories, another scholar could easily argue that another one is better. The statement is too confident. The student should not use the word 'best' and should explain why this theory is useful.

> Students are very weak in their basic mathematical knowledge due to over-dependence on calculators.

This is the student's opinion, but she cannot write this without evidence. She could cite studies that have shown this to be true, or she could adjust her language: 'Some students' mathematical knowledge may suffer because of their over-dependence on calculators.'

A way to ensure academic modesty is to use cautious language. This is also called 'hedging' language, because 'to hedge against something' means to protect yourself from its consequences.

> In order to encourage consumers to try their goods for the first time, a number of promotional methods should be applied as follows: (...)

The student says that the company 'should' do something, where he should really have made a suggestion ('could').

> The next step is to conduct a long-term observation among the workers to find out if they show a more creative and conscientious approach in their daily work.

Here, 'is' is too strong. The student is saying what he thinks is a good idea, so it really is a suggestion. He could have used 'may be' or 'could be'.

For more information on cautious language, see Chapter 8.

A common mistake that students make is to use cautious language where it is not necessary. They use 'would', 'might', 'likely to', etc. because they have learnt that these verbs are common in academic writing.

> Annual financial reports might include information from financial statements and other sources.

Glossary

shareholder
(shareholders)
N-COUNT
A shareholder
is a person who
owns shares in a
company.

stakeholder
(stakeholders)
N-COUNT
Stakeholders
are people who
have an interest
in a company's
or organization's
affairs.

creditor
(creditors)
N-COUNT
Your creditors
are the people
who you owe
money to.

Even without knowing much about the subject, we can assume that the purpose of financial reports is to give financial information. The verb 'might' needs to be taken out of the sentence.

It would come across as immodest if your essay were to state 'I did ..., I did ..., I did ...'. Even if you use the 'we' form, this would not improve matters much. It is possible to use 'I' and 'we' in certain circumstances, however.

For more information on when it is appropriate to use 'I' and 'we', see Chapter 8.

Here though, we will work on the basis that 'I' and 'we' should be avoided where possible and we will be looking at examples of writing where language is used that is not objective enough.

> As we all know, an enterprise is composed of many different groups, including management (such as the board of directors, the Chief Executive Officer, other executives), shareholders, and other influential stakeholders (including lenders, suppliers, employees, creditors, customers and the community).

This is an interesting one: the student is including the reader by saying 'we', so she is making her comment quite personal and suggesting that if readers do not know there may be something wrong with them. We can say the same thing but make it more impersonal: 'It is commonly known that an enterprise ...'

> In my opinion, the company should do this, because it would offer direct business benefits.

The student could say 'If the company did this, they would receive direct business benefits.' There is normally no need to say 'in my opinion' as your whole essay is a development of your opinion.

For more information on developing a clear point of view, see Chapter 8.

> Non-shareholder stakeholders also play an important role in corporate governance. As I mentioned before, stakeholders include employees, suppliers, local communities and local governments.

Here, 'I' can easily be left out, so it is best to do so.

Clarity

If your writing has clarity, it means that you have expressed yourself clearly and there is no doubt about what you mean.

Your choice of words needs to be specific and precise.

> This could help stakeholders to understand the health of public companies, by means of a Balance Sheet, Income Statement, Statement of Changes in Financial Position and other descriptions.

It is not clear what the student means by the word 'descriptions', as he seems to be referring to financial information.

> We now need to consider how enterprises perform successfully. In my opinion, good corporate governance is the main reason.

At first sight the two sentences don't seem to relate as the words 'how' and 'reason' do not connect with each other. With careful rereading it becomes clearer that the student is saying that good corporate governance is the main reason why enterprises that operate successfully manage to do so. An improvement here would be 'In the next section we will consider the reasons why enterprises are successful and the central role of good corporate governance.'

> The first one depends on the situation: they may need to change the leader if his style is not suitable.

The student has chosen 'his' but this cannot be what she wanted to say, as leaders can be male or female. She probably did not want to write 'his or her' because that is quite awkward. However, there are other solutions: 'companies may need to change leaders if their style is not suitable', or 'a company may need to change its leader if their style is not suitable'. The plural can be used to refer to a singular person in this type of sentence.

> In short, there are always two sides to every coin.

It is tempting to use sayings, as they often express exactly what you want to say in few words. However, they are best used when speaking, not in formal writing. In this example, the saying is used as the conclusion of

Glossary

saying (sayings)
N-COUNT
A saying is a
sentence that
people often
say and that
gives advice or
information
about human life
and experience.

a paragraph, but this is a poor ending. The main reason for not using sayings is that they tend to express universal truths or commonly held beliefs, and therefore do not demonstrate original, research-based or critical thinking. They are also often used in speech, which makes them sound informal.

> In confusing the role of author, editor, etc. Diba refers to the multiplicity of the text.

The abbreviation 'etc.' is not very common in academic text, because it forces the reader to come up with more examples themselves. Academic writers need to be clear and precise. Here it is hard to imagine what other roles the writer is referring to.

> The steam engine was a reliable power source at that time and used in mining, cotton, railways, etc.

If the steam engine was only used in mining, cotton and railways, then the student should simply have put a full stop rather than 'etc'., but there are probably more examples to be given. Here, an improvement would be: '... used in mining, cotton, railways and other industries.'

> There are many things that need to be taken into consideration.

The word 'thing' is very imprecise, and there is never a need to use it. Simply say what it stands for. Here, the word 'factors' could be used. Other vague words and phrases to avoid include 'kind of' and 'stuff'.

Exercise 3

Replace 'thing' in these sentences with a more specific word or phrase.

1 Non-verbal behaviour has significant effects on every living thing.

2 This environment is non-living things like rocks, water and air.

3 It is necessary from a social point of view to talk about unimportant things sometimes.

4 Giving pupils more responsibilities during an already stressful time may not be the wisest thing to do.

5 Stress may not be as negative a thing for our health as previously thought.

Tip

Tip ✓ If you are an international student, you may worry that you might make more mistakes than native speakers, but everyone makes mistakes. The key is to try your hardest to avoid them. Careful proofreading will raise the standards of your work.

Glossary

sub-clause
(sub-clauses)
N-COUNT
A sub-clause or subordinate clause is a clause in a sentence which adds to or completes the information given in the main clause. It cannot usually stand alone as a sentence.

dense (denser, densest) ADJ
If a text or sentence is dense, it contains a lot of information in a small or short space.

We have already talked about the need for clear structure and guidance in Chapters 2 and 3. Organization is a very important aspect of clarity.

Some students think that academic language is more difficult, and they therefore attempt to write very long sentences with many sub-clauses, passives and other constructions which are quite complex.

It is true that academic sentences are quite long in comparison to some other written genres. They can also look quite dense, because using a lot of nouns means including a lot of information in a short space.

It may take you some time to get used to the level of difficulty in the texts that you read. However, when you are writing, the principle of clarity is more important than considerations of length or complexity.

For information on the academic principle of Accuracy, see Chapter 5.

As a writer, if you write too many impersonal constructions, passives, noun phrases and long sentences, you will make it harder for your reader. The most important aspect of academic writing is the reader. They will prefer a variety of constructions and sentence lengths. They will also prefer a shorter, simple sentence that is easy to understand to a complex one which does not make much sense or is full of mistakes.

In this chapter we have looked at a number of language issues to avoid. It is not a full list, but you don't need one. By doing research, you will see what others do and learn from them.

For information on the academic principle of Authority, see Chapter 8, and for information on the academic principle of Integrity, see Chapter 9.

Tip

Tip ✓ Focus on the academic principles (e.g. 'be modest'), not the individual guidelines ('use "may"'). Observe how others write: each time you read an article, think about its style in relation to the academic principles. This way, you will develop a better 'feel' for academic writing and you will find yourself automatically making the right language choices.

Exercise 4

Rewrite the following paragraph to make it more academic:

Children who are of school age should do a lot of practice at home by working on their skills and by practising and solving a large number of mathematics problems. We should only allow them to use a calculator when they want to find out what the answer to the problems was. Sometimes, when they do a long calculation, the calculator should also be used because not many students would be able to do it without one. The impact of this practising is to help them to improve their knowledge and not always to rely on the calculator all the time!

Remember

✓ The same academic principles – formality, efficiency, modesty and clarity – matter in your essays as before, but at university you need to be more aware of them and they are even more important.

✓ Formality – use a formal, academic style.

✓ Efficiency – avoid repetition of phrases and ideas; careful proofreading is essential.

✓ Modesty – the language needs to be impersonal and cautious where appropriate.

✓ Clarity – although some academic authors write texts that may be considered complex, you are expected to write essays that express your ideas clearly and precisely.

5 | Accuracy

Aims
- ✓ improve accuracy
- ✓ choose the correct tense
- ✓ focus on subject-verb agreement
- ✓ use punctuation correctly
- ✓ use articles correctly
- ✓ become aware of common errors

Quiz
Self-evaluation

For each statement below, circle the word which is true for you.

1	I always check the tense of the verbs I have used in an essay before submitting it.	agree │ disagree │ not sure
2	I know how to check for subject-verb agreement.	agree │ disagree │ not sure
3	I can use punctuation correctly in my essays.	agree │ disagree │ not sure
4	I feel confident about when and when not to use the articles 'a' and 'the' in my writing.	agree │ disagree │ not sure
5	I am aware of common errors and how to avoid them.	agree │ disagree │ not sure

The academic principle of Accuracy

Glossary

accuracy
N-UNCOUNT
The accuracy of information or measurements is their quality of being true or correct, even in small details.

As we said in Chapter 4, accuracy is considered important in all types of academic writing, and it is even more of an issue when your writing is being assessed. An essay which includes avoidable language mistakes and looks like a draft will annoy your reader, and may even prevent them from understanding what you are trying to say.

Tenses

Choosing the correct tense for the verb in your sentence can be difficult. There is more about this in Chapter 10. Here, we focus on accuracy.

The following tenses are wrong. Read the examples and think about why they are wrong.

---

1 ✗ According to these documents, the council **has considering** it since the 1980s.

2 ✗ They demonstrated that the council **had communicating** its intentions before 1982.

3 ✗ Their engineers **were draw up** the plans as far back as 1984.

4 ✗ Normally, the tourist market **will been** more **affected** in an economic recession.

5 ✗ In this essay, the Human Fertilization and Embryology Act 1990 **will be consider** from different points of view.

The simplest answer is that these forms don't exist, e.g. 'has considered' or 'has been considering' are possible combinations, but 'has considering' is not.

Subject-verb agreement

A common error is a lack of agreement between the subject and the verb. The verb needs to 'match' or 'agree with' its subject, e.g. it is 'I believe', 'the director believes', 'they believe'. Look at the examples. The subjects are <u>underlined</u> and the verbs are highlighted.

✗ First of all, <u>the company</u> need to interview the employees who have been involved in the training programme and gather feedback about the course from them.

✓ First of all, <u>the company</u> needs to interview the employees who have been involved in the training programme and gather feedback about the course from them.

✗ <u>Sales</u> of sweets and other types of junk food has decreased throughout the country because of successful national campaigns.

✓ <u>Sales</u> of sweets and other types of junk food have decreased throughout the country because of successful national campaigns.

Subjects and objects often consist of nouns or noun phrases. The verb needs to agree with the most important word in the subject, the head noun. In order to find this, you need to be aware of the construction of noun phrases.

Nouns are often pre-modified or post-modified, i.e. they are described by words that come before them and after them.

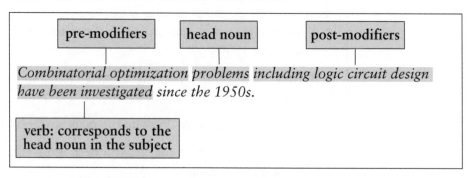

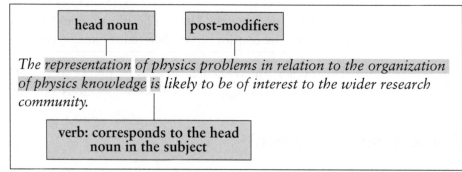

 Exercise 1

Find the head noun in the subject and choose the corresponding form of the verb.

1   Complex and currently unresolved issues arising in research on innovation in complex organizations **is / are** also to be examined.

2   Lastly, a possible solution of the horizon, flatness, homogeneity and isotropy problems in cosmology **is / are** suggested.

3   Hundreds of reliable focal-mechanism solutions for deep and intermediate depth earthquakes **was / were** analysed.

For more information on how to identify the verb and the subject, see Chapter 7.

Punctuation

Glossary

defining relative clause (defining relative clauses)
N-COUNT
A defining relative clause is a subordinate clause which gives information about a person or thing, explaining or specifying which person or thing you are talking about.

Punctuation can be important as it has an effect on the reader's perception of a piece of text.

Occasionally, a small change in punctuation can affect the meaning of a sentence, as in the following examples:

> 1 In high-risk patients, who attain large benefits from treatment, expensive drugs may be cost effective.
>
> 2 In high-risk patients who attain large benefits from treatment, expensive drugs may be cost effective.

In sentence 1 the writer says that all high-risk patients attain large benefits from treatment. The clause 'who attain large benefits from treatment' is put between commas and is a non-defining relative clause that gives extra information. If you read the sentence without the extra information, you can really see how the information applies to all high-risk patients: 'In high-risk patients expensive drugs may be cost effective.'

Sentence 2 means that expensive drugs may be cost effective only for those high-risk patients who attain large benefits. The clause 'who attain large benefits from treatment' is not preceded by a comma and is a defining relative clause. There is no 'extra' information, just essential information, so you cannot read the sentence without the relative clause.

In most cases, punctuation does not have such a great effect on meaning. However, it can have a very negative impact on the reader if it is used incorrectly. For example, the reader may be annoyed if there are too many basic errors.

The reader may also be confused if the clarity of the text is affected by the way punctuation is used. The following is an example of a sentence that goes on for too long.

> ✗ There is also a problem with the sales, despite the attractive low prices, sales are heavily dependent on the season.
>
> ✓ There is also a problem with the sales. Despite the attractive low prices, sales are heavily dependent on the season.

Tip ✓ If you are not sure about punctuation, read the relevant section out loud. If there is a natural pause in the sentence, you probably need a comma. Longer pauses are represented by a full stop.

Glossary

abbreviation
(abbreviations)
N-COUNT
An abbreviation is a short form of a word or phrase, made by leaving out some of the letters or by using only the first letter of each word.

possession
N-UNCOUNT
Possession is the state of having something because you have obtained it or because it belongs to you.

Punctuation is a large area, and there is not enough room here to describe all its aspects. However, here are some guidelines for the use of punctuation in academic English.

Sentences that can stand on their own are separated by a full stop. Full stops are also used in abbreviations after letters that are not the last letter of the word.	.
Sentences that can stand on their own but have a strong link can be separated by a semi-colon. Semi-colons are also used in longer lists that include commas.	;
Items in lists, parts of sentences, extra information and some adverbs are often separated by commas.	,
Lists, long quotes and explanations are often preceded by a colon.	:
Possession is indicated by an apostrophe.	'
If you are adding your own words into a quote, you should use square brackets.	[ ]
Additional information can be given between round brackets (but do not do this too often in academic English).	( )
Capital letters are used at the beginning of sentences and proper names.	A,B, ... instead of a, b, ...
When you omit words from a quotation, use ellipsis.	...
Exact or special words are indicated by single quotation marks.	' '
In British English, when you quote within a quote, you use double quotation marks.	" "
Special concepts or titles can be indicated by italics.	*italics*

Some students are not clear about the distinctions between the use of colons, semi-colons and commas in sentences. Here are some examples of the use of these punctuation marks in academic English.

Semi-colons (;) are used between sentences that can stand independently:

■ to distinguish different parts of series that contain commas

> *There are three areas that interest us: the introductory part, with its introduction of the topic, its generalizations and definitions; the middle part, which can have subdivisions, different patterns or structures; and finally, the conclusion.*

■ when you connect two sentences that are closely related in meaning without using a connecting word

> *Some customers preferred source code; others wanted to continue with pre-packaged product binaries.*

■ when two independent sentences are connected with a transition signal

> *Some customers did not want to use source code; therefore most manufacturers kept producing pre-packaged product binaries too.*

Colons (:) draw the reader's attention to the next words:

■ to introduce a list

> *We will look at essay structure: introductions, main body and conclusion.*
>
> Note that we do not use a colon after a verb:
>
> ✗ *The reasons that are most often cited are: resistance and intolerance.*
>
> ✓ *The reasons that are most often cited are resistance and intolerance.*

■ to introduce a subtitle

> *Treatment of asthma in children: a critical analysis*

■ before direct quotations and in some citations

> *As Farb (2011: 32) states: 'You have to act quickly. The longer you draw out one of these crises and let it drag on, the weaker you get.'*
>
> *Farb (2011: 32)*

Commas (,) are very common within sentences, but be careful not to use them instead of full stops between independent sentences. Commas are used:

- in reference lists

> *Shida, K. and Nanno, M., 2008. Probiotics and immunology: separating the wheat from the chaff. Trends Immunol. 29: 565–573*

- in some citations, numbers and dates

> *(McCarthy, 2010)*
>
> *13,500,000*
>
> *on 23 September, 2013*

- between items in a series of more than two (note: in British English not before 'and', but in American usage also before 'and')

> *A PEST analysis looks at the political, economic, social and technological aspects of a situation.*

- with certain transition signals (e.g. use one after *in fact, for example, however,* but not after *despite, even though*)

> *Moreover, all principles and theorems of inductive logic are analytic.*

- to separate parts of sentences but not whole sentences

> *Despite the attractive low prices, sales are heavily dependent on the season.*

- before *and, but, so, or* when they connect clauses

> *These databases provide a widely used source of data for health care research, but their accuracy remains uncertain.*

- to separate non-essential information

> *Allergic asthma, which is present in as many as 10% of individuals in industrialized nations, is characterized amongst other symptoms by chronic airway inflammation.*

possessive
(possessives)
N-COUNT
A possessive
is a word such
as 'my' or 'his'
which shows
who or what
something
belongs to or is
connected with,
or the possessive
form of a name
or noun which
has 's added to it,
as in 'Jenny's' or
'cat's'.

Apostrophes (') are confusing for many writers. Here is an overview of their use in possessive forms.

's is used to express possession. It is put immediately after the noun it refers to. For example:

> *the committee's decision*
>
> *the men's decision*

If the noun already ends in *s*, the apostrophe is used on its own. For example:

> *both committees' decisions*
>
> *Jones' decision (Jones's decision is also correct)*

Note that pronouns do not have an apostrophe: *s* is simply added to a word to form *yours, hers, its, ours, theirs*.

The form *it's* exists, but it is the contraction for *it is*.

Notice the use of full stops (.) in the following commonly used abbreviations in academic English:

cf. compare	ibid. in the book or article already mentioned
ch. Chapter	
e.g. for example	n.d. no date available
ed. editor (but no full stop in eds: editors)	no. number
	para. paragraph
et al. and others	p. page
etc. and so forth	pp. pages
fig. figure	viz. namely, that is to say
i.e. that is	vol. volume

Exercise 2

Add the punctuation to the following paragraph. The first two have been done.

To begin with, it is essential to understand what the feminist approach is, why it has emerged and what its positions are according to saratankos (2005 71) the feminist approach is defined as an established type of research which has the specific purpose of studying women and their status in the community put differently women are the dominant research subject of the feminist approach which aims at attaining economic social and political equality between the sexes emancipating women and increasing peoples understanding of blatant sexism

Articles

Glossary

determiner
(determiners)
N-COUNT
A determiner is a word which is used at the beginning of a noun group to indicate, for example, which thing you are referring to or whether you are referring to one thing or several. Common English determiners are 'a', 'the', 'some', 'this', and 'each'.

demonstrative adjective
(demonstrative adjectives)
N-COUNT
Demonstrative adjectives are the words 'this', 'that', 'these', and 'those'.

Knowing when to use the articles *a(n)* or *the* and when not to use an article is very difficult for most non-native speakers.

There are too many rules to memorize and too many exceptions to them, so in this section we will focus on what is most important. As always, it is the impact on your reader you need to think about. Occasionally the incorrect use of articles can cause confusion, so it is important to try to get it right. More commonly, mistakes with articles are likely to be annoying for the reader, especially if they seem to be basic mistakes. We are therefore going to focus on the main rules about articles.

1 You cannot have a singular countable noun in your text without something preceding it.

Check your work for singular words that are countable in their context. You will either need to put them in the plural form or put something in front of them – an article ('a' or 'the') or other determiner (possessives such as 'my', demonstrative adjectives such as 'this', quantity words such as 'each').

✗ *Tube needed to be labelled.*

✓ *Each tube needed to be labelled.* ✓ *The tube needed to be labelled.*

2 If you put an article in front of a singular noun, decide between 'a' or 'the'.

Use 'the' to refer to something known or specific, e.g. something that has been mentioned before or something that is defined immediately afterwards.

✗ *The tubes needed to be labelled with a name provided.*

✓ *The tubes needed to be labelled with the name provided.*

3 Check that plural forms are preceded by 'the' if they refer to something specific.

> ✗ *Tubes used in this experiment were labelled 'T1', 'T2', T3', and so on.*
>
> ✓ *The tubes used in this experiment were labelled 'T1', 'T2', T3', and so on.*

Let's apply this to the following paragraph. First of all, we have highlighted all the singular nouns (excluding proper names):

> Many researchers have started to investigate the role of social media in crisis communications. With more and more people on sites such as Facebook, Twitter and YouTube, technology has fundamentally changed the way people connect with each other and how they communicate. Compared to traditional media platform, social media enjoy the advantages of low cost, fast information sharing and more opportunities to communicate even globally (Wright and Hinson, 2009). More importantly, this information can be shared by a large number of people quickly or even in real time without the work of journalist (Colley and Collier, 2009). This can be extremely toxic for companies when they are facing major crisis. On the other hand, if companies can handle it well, there are benefits to be found in crisis management. (Veil, Buehner and Palenchar, 2011).

The singular, countable nouns are: *role, way, platform, number, journalist, crisis.*

Note that the others are nouns that don't have a plural form in this context (*technology, information, time, work, management*) or words that are part of fixed expressions where we cannot make a change to the use of the articles (it is always 'on <u>the</u> other **hand**').

The student has correctly included the following articles with the countable nouns:

'the' role: we know what 'role' specifically refers to ('of social media')

'the' way: this specifically refers to the way in which people connect with each other

'a' number: we know this is about a number of people, but it does not refer to a specific group of people.

However, the student cannot leave the other three countable nouns without determiners.

- platform: this would work better in the sentence as the plural form because the media has more than one platform: *platforms.*

- journalist: this should be the plural, *journalists*, as they are not talking about a particular journalist, or they could say '*a journalist*', in which 'a' refers to any journalist.

- crisis: this is likely to refer to one crisis at a time, so the plural form does not work so well. 'A' is the correct article here, again because it could refer to 'any' crisis; the idea of a crisis is being introduced.

If you make it a habit to check the singular countable nouns in your essays as you write, you are likely to avoid some of the mistakes that look basic to native speakers and might annoy your reader.

Tip ✓ If you are not sure if something is known/specific or not, check if you could list it. If you can, then it is specific and you need to use 'the'.

For example, you would use 'the' in the first example below, because you could name the projects (underlined), but you would not use 'the' in the second sentence because it would be impossible to list them all.

1 The <u>other research projects in the Biosciences department at Birmingham University</u> ...
2 <u>Other research projects in Bioscience departments in the country</u> ...

Common errors

Glossary

respectively
ADV
Respectively means in the same order as the items that you have just mentioned.

The following are some more examples of incorrect language use, taken from student essays, which may have a negative effect on the reader.

Sentence structure	These sentences have two main verbs where there should only be one. The solution is to split them into two separate sentences (or two clauses linked with a coordinator such as 'and') or to use a main clause and a sub-clause in the sentence:
✗ *The government should help with education should be obligatory until the age of 18.*	
✗ *School should be obligatory until the age of 18 is very important for everyone.*	✓ *The government should help with education **by making it obligatory** until the age of 18.*
	✓ *School should be obligatory until the age of 18 **as education is** very important.*
Prepositions	✓ *There are many **reasons for** adopting an immediate strategy.*
✗ *There are many **reasons of** adopting an immediate strategy.*	
✗ *Doctors and patients regularly need to **discuss about** routine clinical decisions.*	✓ *Doctors and patients regularly need to **discuss** routine clinical decisions.*

Connectors	In informal written English (e.g. emails), people often start a sentence with 'But', 'So', 'And' or 'Because' to relate a sentence to the preceding one. In academic English, it is better to use 'However', 'Therefore', 'Additionally' and 'This is because' respectively. Another solution, which is better in the case of short sentences, is to create one sentence instead of two:
✗ *In an ideal situation, students would work long-term with a native speaker. But this is just not possible for whole classes.*	
✗ *It would not be a practical solution for dehydration. Because of its excessively salty taste.*	✓ *In an ideal situation, students would work long-term with a native speaker, but this is just not possible for whole classes.*
	✓ *It would not be a practical solution for dehydration because of its excessively salty taste.*
	Note that you can use some of these words at the start of the sentence but they must relate to what comes after and not to the previous sentence:
	✓ *Because of its excessively salty taste, it would not be a practical solution for dehydration.*

Tip ✓ It is important to identify which types of common errors you might typically make, and try to avoid them. Although these can be different for each individual, be aware of the types of errors that are often made by speakers of your first language. For example, Chinese speakers are more likely to choose wrong word combinations (e.g. ✗ *suffer from critical problems*, ✗ *develop new customers*), whereas Arabic speakers are more likely to forget the verb 'to be' (e.g. ✗ *Marketers who prepared generally perform better*, instead of ✓ *Marketers who are prepared generally perform better*).

Remember

Check your work for:

✓ correct tense choice

✓ subject-verb agreement

✓ correct use of punctuation

✓ correct use of the articles 'a(n)' and 'the', including whether or not you actually need to use an article

✓ common errors.

6 | Research and analysis

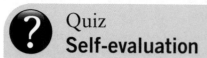

Aims ✓ develop research skills
      ✓ identify suitable sources
      ✓ develop note-making skills
      ✓ decide on level of detail and what is relevant
      ✓ develop critical thinking skills

? Quiz
Self-evaluation

For each statement below, circle the word which is true for you.

1	I prefer to decide what my answer to an essay question is while I carry out my research.	agree | disagree | not sure
2	I know how to identify suitable sources.	agree | disagree | not sure
3	I feel confident about how to take notes.	agree | disagree | not sure
4	I know how to decide how much research I need to do and what information is relevant to include.	agree | disagree | not sure
5	I know how to demonstrate that I can think critically in my writing.	agree | disagree | not sure

Research skills

Glossary

reliable ADJ
Information that is reliable or that is from a reliable source is very likely to be correct.

Once you have got your first outline, you can start your research. Don't look for every book or article related to your general topic. Instead, you need to search for resources in the library and online to find answers to the **specific** questions your essay needs to address. This stops you wasting time and will help you to make your essay more focused. You will need to:

- identify reliable resources that cover the specific areas you need to write about

- note down the full details of the resources

- read the useful sections only

- make clear notes.

Glossary

tentative ADJ
Tentative answers, plans, or arrangements are not definite or certain, but have been given or made as a first step.

initiative
(initiatives)
N-COUNT
An initiative is an important act or statement that is intended to solve a problem.

Doing this involves a variety of skills.

Have your essay question and outline with you when you do the research. This way you will keep your research purpose in mind.

It is very important to try and decide what your answer to the question is BEFORE you start on the research. You can use this tentative answer to guide your research; ultimately it will help you organize your essay better and make a stronger argument.

For example:

Critically assess car speed reduction initiatives in the UK countryside and determine the way forward.	
Introduction	■ the problem of traffic speed: consequences ■ the particular issues in the countryside
Main body	■ a description of the different initiatives so far ■ for each initiative: a discussion of its strengths, weaknesses and ultimate success, with examples and other evidence ■ mention the current and predicted traffic situation and future speed reduction plans
Conclusion	■ answers to the questions: Which initiative has worked best so far? Can it be continued? ■ recommendations

Before you start looking for sources, you should ask yourself what you already know, e.g. consider what you have learnt in lectures. What initiatives do you know? What has worked in your country or local area? What would you like to see done more often and why?

If you can answer these questions, you have developed a **line of argument** for your essay and given yourself a **focus** for your research.

In this example, you may know about vehicle-activated signs (flashing lights that remind drivers of the speed limit and let them know that they are going too fast), but you have noticed that even though they go off all the time, people seem to ignore them. You think that the same is true for normal signs and reminders. Imagine that you feel passionately about the countryside. You would want to emphasize that the countryside is different to the city, and that initiatives that work in urban areas should not just be transferred to the countryside: it needs its own solutions.

You would not want anything spoiling the look of the countryside, yet you would want traffic to go slowly. You would therefore be in favour of anything that works but is not highly visible, and you have heard of places where they make the road seem narrower, e.g. by using different colours for footpaths.

Without doing this thinking first, your essay might have looked like a description of what schemes exist and what evidence there is to show that they work. Now that you have a line of argument for the whole essay it will be a lot stronger: you will argue that the countryside is a special place which needs appropriate initiatives. This will help you formulate criteria so that you can critically assess the existing initiatives.

You now also have a focus for your research. Rather than listing the initiatives that you read about, you can organize them as soon as you find them. These ideas could look like this, with the ideas you already had in bold:

General initiatives	Initiatives that may be particularly suitable for the countryside

■ **vehicle-activated signs**
■ **speed limit reminders**
■ 30 mph speed limits
■ cameras
■ speed bumps and rumble strips
■ traffic islands and mini-roundabouts
■ detection
	■ all speed limit signs on wooden posts
	■ removing road markings
	■ making the road appear narrower
	  – **different colours for footpaths**
	  – putting bushes closer to the edge
	■ 20 mph speed limits in villages
	■ community police presence

In your essay, you might want to talk about the general initiatives first, discussing their strengths and weaknesses, before looking at initiatives that work best in the countryside.

Suitable sources

Before you start looking for sources, consider what you already have. Apart from some ideas of your own, you may have lecture notes, textbooks, and recommended sources on the reading list for your module. If a book is on your reading list, this does not mean that you have to read all of it, but that there are sections of it which will be useful for your module.

Glossary

pedagogy
N-UNCOUNT
Pedagogy is the study and theory of the methods and principles of teaching.

synonym
(synonyms)
N-COUNT
A synonym is a word or expression which means the same as another word or expression.

authoritative ADJ
Someone or something that is authoritative has a lot of knowledge of a particular subject.

For this particular essay you will need examples of traffic initiatives. You may find information from local councils online. You could also look at sources from organizations that promote the countryside or that work to prevent road accidents. Textbooks might be useful for information about traffic speed problems in general. You will also need statistics about traffic initiatives and road accidents; there may be studies about this in academic journals.

Use your online library catalogue to look for more books and journals by entering a key word related to your essay. Have a look at the following essay question and decide which search terms you would enter in the library catalogue before you read on.

> *How can an understanding of sociology contribute to the development of effective pedagogies in physical education and sport?*

The key words in the question itself are 'sociology', 'development', 'pedagogies', 'physical education' and 'sport'. On their own, they would generate many resources but they are likely to be too general. Entering them as combinations will lead to better results, e.g. 'sports pedagogies', 'sports sociology', 'physical education pedagogies'. Also think of synonyms and different word forms to do your searches, e.g. 'exercise' and 'pedagogy' could be useful here.

Your lecturer or librarian will also tell you about electronic databases. You may need a password for these, after which you will have access to more resources that are related to your discipline. You can then look at the different issues of a journal and do a search for your particular essay topic.

You also need to decide which sources are reliable. Academic writing needs to be authoritative. Your writing can only be reliable if the sources that you have used are trustworthy.

For more information about the academic principle of Authority, see Chapter 8.

To determine if a source can be used, ask yourself what the purpose of the original text was, and what your purpose is. If you study English and want to analyse the type of language that companies use, then company websites are the right source. However, if you are a business student writing an analysis of an aspect of a company, then a company website is unlikely to be helpful. Instead, you would look at the company's annual report as well as other independent sources.

Writing

Websites are not more or less reliable than printed sources. The annual report that was just mentioned would look exactly the same online as it does in print. However, websites do not always give their authors' names and even when we do know, they may not be an authority in their field. They may therefore not be reliable enough.

Wikipedia is not considered an academic source, because anyone can change information about a certain topic. This is its strength in many ways, as people are building knowledge together and responding to what is current, but often the information is not complete or accurate enough. The contributions are anonymous and some of them are wrong, sometimes deliberately. The other reason that Wikipedia is not academic is that its purpose is not the same as yours: it tries to inform the general public, whereas you are writing for scholars. You cannot use the site as a source for your academic writing, but it can be useful to get an overview of a topic and some ideas about other sources that might be more trustworthy.

Printed encyclopedias are more reliable, because a publisher was prepared to print the information. However, the information is likely to be too general for your academic purpose (in the same way that dictionaries are). Moreover, knowledge changes very quickly, so the information may no longer be correct.

If **books and journals** are published you can trust them because the information was checked before publication. Some online sources look trustworthy, e.g. because they present themselves as a journal, but you still need to double check. Look on the site for publisher's information, the name of the authors and other information. If you can't find any, then certainly don't trust the site. The website address can give you some clues: if it ends in 'ac.uk' it was authored by a higher or further education institution in the UK, 'gov' is a government website, 'sch' a school, 'co' or 'com' a company.

It is not always necessary to read primary (= original) sources, rather than secondary sources (= those that report the original research). However, it is a good habit to get into: if the original source is important in your discipline, then you really should have read it. Also, if you are working at postgraduate level, then you are expected to read the primary sources.

If all your sources were published decades ago, you have probably not been reading widely enough. You need a variety of sources, but recent ones are particularly important, as they will reflect current thinking. As always, your purpose is important – a historian will of course need to examine older texts.

> **Tip** ✓ Google Scholar (http://www. scholar. google. com) is a search engine that looks for academic sources rather than general sources. Although you should still check that these are reliable, using this tool is a good place to start if you are looking for a journal article on a particular topic. It has a particularly large database of medical sources.

Once you have identified the relevant sources, you can start reading.

Note-making skills

First of all, you need to write down the bibliographic information of each source: the author's surname and initials, the full title, the publisher, the year of publication, the place of publication, and sometimes the chapter or pages. For books this information is on one of the first pages when you open it. Because of the academic principles of Authority – where you show that you have knowledge about the subject so can be trusted – and Accuracy, you need to focus on the details and copy everything correctly. Get into the habit of doing this first, as you don't want to forget and have to look up the details again when you are writing your essay.

For more information about the data you need for each type of source, see Chapter 9.

> **Tip** ✓ Create a separate document in which you put all the bibliographic data of your sources. This can then be tidied up when you put your reference list together.

Exercise 1

The following information was found by a student of theology. Did she copy enough information and is it correct? Make the necessary changes to the column on the right.

Source information	Student's notes
Article	
Trauma, Transference and 'Working through' in Writing the History of the 'Shoah'	**Article title**: Trauma, Transferrence and 'Working through' in Writing the History of the Shoah
Saul Friedlander	**Author**: Friedlander, S.
History and Memory Vol. 4, No. 1 (Spring – Summer, 1992), pp. 39–59 Published by: Indiana University Press	**Journal**: History and Memory, Volume 4, No. 1, 1992, Indiana Press
Book	
The Democratic Ideal and the Shoah: The Unthought in Political Modernity	**Book title**: The Democratic Ideal and the Shoah; the unthought in political modernity
Trigano, Shmuel	**Authors**: Samuel Trigano, Eileen Mehann
Production by Eileen Mehann	**Publisher**: State University of New York Press, Albany
Marketing by Fran Keneston	
Published by: State University of New York Press, Albany	
2009 State University of New York	

Tips ✓ Names can be difficult. One issue is that you may not know whether the name you find is the author's surname or first name, especially if they are foreign names for you. If the names are separated by a comma, then the first name you read is the surname. If you really cannot work it out, look up the author's books online, e.g. check via Google Scholar if academic authors have cited the same source in their reference lists. You can then cite the sources in the same way.

✓ Another issue can come up when you need to refer in your text to an author as 'he' or 'she'; you may not be certain about the gender of an author if it is a foreign name for you. Make a note when a source refers to another author as 'he' or 'she' – this information may be very useful when you are writing the essay.

Tips

Glossary

paraphrasing
N-UNCOUNT
Paraphrasing
is when you
express what
someone else has
said or written in
a different way.

spidergram
(spidergrams)
N-COUNT
A spidergram
is a drawing to
show facts or
ideas, which has
the main topic
in a circle in
the centre with
other important
facts on lines
drawn out from
this central
circle.

Making notes about content is both a reading and a writing skill. It helps you while reading because it makes you concentrate and think about what the text means and why it is important.

Do not copy the author's language, but use your own words to summarize what they have said. This is an important part of the paraphrasing process. When you do write down the exact words of the original text, so that you can quote them later, make sure you note the page numbers (and the bibliographical data) as you will need those in your essay. It is important that you make it very clear in your notes which are your words and which are quotes.

There are different ways of making notes. This can vary from making a small comment in the margin to using a new page to visually represent the structure of the text. Don't start making notes in the first reading stage, but wait until you are ready to do more detailed reading, otherwise you may make too many notes and include irrelevant information.

Most people have a preferred note-making style. However, you need to keep your purpose in mind and ask yourself which types of notes would be best. You will save a lot of time when you are writing the essay if you have chosen the best format to present the information. Here are some questions to help you decide:

- what will I use these notes for? (e.g. paraphrasing, quoting, summarizing)

- am I likely to need notes from the whole text or just certain sections?

- can the text easily be represented visually? (e.g. a table with two parts for advantages and disadvantages, a flow chart for the explanation of processes, a spidergram for topics with many subdivisions, a timeline for chronological information or other sequences, linear notes (with title, subtitles and numbers) to show which items are more important than others)

For more information on paraphrasing, see Chapter 10.

Exercise 2

Read the following text. Look at the questions above to help you decide what types of notes would be best. Shorten the text, use abbreviations and symbols, and use your own words. Compare your notes with the ones in the Answer key.

A group of climate scientists and engineers from the UK's Royal Society are investigating a number of ideas to solve the climate change problem. One idea is to put giant mirrors into space to reflect sunlight away from the Earth. Another is to put tiny particles into the Earth's atmosphere to block the Sun's energy. Yet another idea is to put iron filings into the ocean to encourage the growth of plankton, which would then absorb carbon dioxide (CO_2) from the atmosphere. However, the research has been criticized because the scientific solutions might discourage individuals from taking responsibility and trying to reduce their carbon dioxide emissions.

There are some standard ways of making notes:

- leave out articles, prepositions (*in, on, …*) and other grammatical words (e.g. 'there is a need for positive experiences in youth sports' could become 'youth sports: need pos. experiences')

- common symbols (e.g. $\because$ for 'because', $\therefore$ for 'therefore', $\rightarrow$ for 'leads to', = for 'equals', < for 'smaller than')

- common abbreviations (e.g. C. for 'century', BC for 'before Christ', e.g. for 'for example')

- discipline-specific abbreviations (e.g. 'CT scan' in medicine, AI for 'artificial intelligence')

- use colour, capitals and other ways to indicate what is important, and leave plenty of white space so that the notes are easier to read and can be added to.

Do use your own symbols and abbreviations as well, but make sure they always mean the same, e.g. if 'div.' stands for 'division' in your notes, it should not have any other meanings (e.g. diversity, dividend, divorce, …).

Making notes is an important part of doing research, especially as many of your notes will be transformed into paraphrases in your essay. The following exercise gives you some more practice.

Tip ✓ To make it easier to remember what your abbreviations of longer words stand for, add the last letter of the word, e.g. 'div^n' (for 'division').

Exercise 3

Rewrite the following text in note form, using bullet points. Follow the information in the tip and use abbreviations where possible. Make a separate note of useful subject-specific language.

> Retailing (the sale of goods from a fixed location) is changing: shopping is becoming a leisure activity as much as a necessity, along with the rise of home delivery services saving time and journeys. Convenience is a powerful motivator for shoppers' behaviour.
>
> During the last two years, independent retailers have struggled more than the chain stores. Research suggests over 12,000 independent stores closed in 2009. Economies of scale (it is cheaper to buy stock in bulk, so big shops can charge lower prices) are one part of the issue. Supermarkets have a stronger control over the supply chain and can manipulate prices more effectively. As a result of the decline in smaller stores, there are now many empty shops in most town centres, some of which have been vacant for some time, and have whitewashed windows.

On a separate page, you may also want to note subject-specific vocabulary to use in your future essays. For example, a student of Business might write down *free enterprise system*, *market forces*, *operating units*, *middle management*. It is important to think about collocations, i.e. common word combinations, and you could also note other academic phrases such as *This is particularly true in the case of ...*, *This framework allows its users to ...*, *These approaches are based on the assumption that ...*

Deciding on level of detail and what is relevant

In addition to knowing how to choose the right sources and deciding on your approach in order to research only what is necessary to answer the question, there other ways to decide what to include.

The word count tells you the level of detail that is needed. If you are required to write a short essay for example, you are not expected to do too much in-depth research, as you will need to come to the point quickly and focus on the most important aspects of the topic.

It can help to imagine the reader as another student, but from a different department. This is an intelligent person who does not know about your topic yet: you need to explain it step by step, making sure you include all the information that is relevant, without repeating yourself.

Critical thinking skills

The word 'critical' has many meanings, one of which is described in the *Collins COBUILD Advanced Dictionary* as follows: 'A critical approach to something involves examining and judging it carefully.' We have already discussed that you have to be critical when you are choosing sources. When you read them, you are then expected to think critically, i.e. question what you read, think logically and draw your own conclusions. Even though you will have selected reliable sources, you may disagree with them. In your essay, you should indicate where you agree and disagree with a particular author.

For example, imagine that you wanted to include a general definition at the start of your essay, but there are many definitions to choose from. You can show that you can think critically by selecting a definition and explaining why you want to use that one. This could be because it is the most cited one, the one most commonly used by other scholars, the most comprehensive one, the one that picks up on aspects related to your specific question, etc. Your justification will demonstrate that you have read widely, understood what you have read, questioned what the authors wrote and thought about how the issues related to your essay question.

Every essay needs to demonstrate your ability to argue, i.e. to put your points across and defend them. Arguing means showing evidence of your critical thinking: weighing up evidence, thinking logically and making your point in a clear and organized way.

It is useful to think about arguments in terms of a three-part structure again.

1   Make your point.

2   Give your evidence.

3   Explain further (e.g. say more about your point or evidence, explain how your evidence supports your point).

The three stages are indicated in the following paragraph from a student essay.

> (1) It is essential for people to learn and understand body language, especially if they have certain jobs or circumstances. (2) For instance, a person who is often in an international environment such as a journalist, business person or diplomat needs to be more careful than a person who works on their own. (3) If a business person travels to a foreign country but does not understand the language there and cannot interpret the body language, this will lead to confusion and embarrassment.

The three stages do not need to be in that order. The student could also have written:

> (2) People whose jobs involve international travel, such as business people, journalists and diplomats may come across difficult situations. (3) They may find themselves in confusing or embarrassing situations if they have travelled to a country where they do not understand the language and cannot interpret the body language. This is why (1) it is essential in certain professions to be able to learn and understand body language.

Note that this example is from a pre-university essay. The stages are often longer in university essays, consisting of more than one sentence.

Exercise 4

Identify the three stages of the argument in the following paragraph. Mark them (1) (point), (2) (evidence) and (3) (explanation).

> Although this approach has been criticized by many researchers who argue that it is not effective enough to teach and learn a second language, it is still useful for teaching spoken English grammar. Firstly, if the teachers want to use this approach to teach features of spoken grammar, they should clearly know what the features of spoken grammar are and have coursebooks based on spoken English grammar. Otherwise, it is very difficult to use this approach in their teaching activity.

A common pattern when arguing is to say what other people's opinions are before saying where you stand. You will have used this technique in previous pieces of writing. Here is an example taken from the start of a pre-university essay.

> Some people take the view that terrorism is the greatest threat that the USA is facing. Others say that global climate change or environmental issues pose the most serious long-term concerns. However, the USA is too vast and powerful for any one source to present much danger.

Notice how the word 'however' indicates the change from the thoughts of others to the opinion that the author wants to develop.

In longer essays this structure is also common, but may be developed over several paragraphs. There could be several paragraphs that develop the thoughts of different authors who look at an issue in one way, followed by paragraphs about those who look at it differently. You will need to make it clear where you stand on the matter.

When you read, you need to be able to follow the author's point of view. One way of doing this is by noticing the counter-argumentation in a text: the common pattern is that first there will be a point of view that has some merit, but is not the one that the author agrees with.

Authors make claims and comment on the ideas of others. Let's have a look at an example of writing by a university student.

> Research has shown that that the mental processing of the internal structure of sentences by learners is affected by many performance factors during real time production (Lyons, 1996). Despite this finding, most research on the development of language ignores the internal structure of processing events, which may be due to a belief that 'comprehension is measured at the end of an utterance, rather than as it is being heard' (Tyler and Marslen-Wilson, 1981: 400). However, it is important to focus on mental processing, as the ability to process the internal structure of sentences influences to a large extent the development of language use in learners' minds as their proficiency increases.

This student agrees with Lyons' finding that mental processing is affected by performance factors. This is clear because he says 'Research has shown'. He then says the finding is ignored and quotes research (from Tyler and Marslen-Wilson) that gives an explanation as to why this is the case. The last sentence has not been attributed to anyone, so it must be his opinion. He explains why it is important that the finding is not ignored.

Even when reading academic and therefore authoritative texts, you should not believe everything. Critical thinking means questioning what you read. Do this as you move through the text.

Let's evaluate the above example. We identified the last sentence as the opinion of the student. He says that the ability to process the internal structure of sentences influences the development of language use in learners' minds as their proficiency increases. Ask yourself: has he provided evidence for the link with proficiency in this paragraph and is it strong evidence? The answer is that he has not provided evidence yet. We will expect to find the evidence in the next paragraph. If it is not provided there, it would be a good idea to make a note about the lack of evidence for this particular point.

Exercise 5

Evaluate the following paragraph as follows:
1   Identify the writer's opinion.
2   Comment on the strength of the evidence.

> Their projects were not effective because of limited budgets of the Trustees and conflicts among small property owners in Halifax who often held the membership of the Trustees (Maslen, 1843; Dalby, 1853). In 1848 the Halifax Municipal Borough Corporation took over the Town Trustees' work. However, this corporation was also restrained by the budget, and it suffered from the conflicts between economists and supporters for social improvement within councillors and aldermen (Ranger, 1851; Iwama, 2003). So, the individual projects raised public awareness of social improvement in the urban environment of Halifax.

Remember

✓   In the research stage, you need to think your own ideas through first, then locate relevant sources.

✓   It is important to choose reliable sources because you will use them to give more authority to your ideas.

✓   You need to select the best type of note organization for each source.

✓   Note-making needs to be systematic: references need to be noted, text needs to be copied or paraphrased with precision, and information from different sources needs to be organized into categories.

✓   The level of depth of your research should be determined by both the word count and the amount of explanation about the topic that an intelligent reader will need.

✓   You are expected to think critically, so always judge your sources carefully. Look for the author's opinions and judge the strength of the evidence. In your essay, explain and justify why you have used the sources.

7 | Reading comprehension

Aims ✓ enhance reading comprehension
      ✓ analyse sentence structure
      ✓ analyse noun phrases
      ✓ identify structural and argumentational signposts

Aims

? Quiz
Self-evaluation

For each statement below, circle the word which is true for you.

1	I can reduce a sentence to its basic parts to understand its meaning.	agree | disagree | not sure
2	I can find what is important information in a sentence and what is not by identifying main subordinate clauses.	agree | disagree | not sure
3	I can work out the meanings of words through an awareness of the different relationships between the nouns in noun combinations.	agree | disagree | not sure
4	I can work out the meanings of words made up of adjective and noun combinations.	agree | disagree | not sure
5	I can identify structural signposts to work out the function of the section of text I am reading.	agree | disagree | not sure
6	I can identify argumentational signposts to see how a section fits into the overall argument the author is making.	agree | disagree | not sure

Analysing sentence structure

Academic language is efficient and a lot is said in few words. This is why academic texts tend to give a lot of information in a short space. When you come across long or difficult sentences during your research, and you think these may be stating an important point that you need to understand and perhaps paraphrase in your essay, reduce them to their basic sentence pattern, and then build them back up, bit by bit.

Look at the following example:

> *Control of immigration to New Zealand is divided into two areas:*
> *visas for temporary stays, such as for tourists or business visits, and*
> *residence permits, which allow a person to settle.*

If we strip the sentences of all the details and look at the underlying grammatical framework, all this is really saying is: 'Control is divided into two areas: A and B.'

We can then think of the extra information bit by bit: **Control** (of immigration to New Zealand) **is divided into two areas:** (A) **visas** (for temporary stays, such as for tourists or business visits) **and** (B) **residence permits** (which allow a person to settle).

As you can increase your comprehension of longer sentences by reducing them to their essentials, it is worth looking at the basic sentence types in English, as shown in these sentences.

1 | subject / verb |
The sea / is calming.

2 | subject / verb / object |
The sea / reflects / the sunshine.

3 | subject / verb / complement |
The sea / is / beautiful.

4 | subject / verb / adverbial |
The sea / glows / in the sunshine.

5 | subject / verb / object / object |
The sea / gives / me / beautiful thoughts.

6 | subject / verb / object / complement |
The sea / has made / people / happy.

7 | subject / verb / object / adverbial |
The sea / offers / different things / at different times.

Note that the different items are not always in that order, and that there could be more adverbials in the sentences.

Look at the following examples:

> *Shopping is becoming a leisure activity as much as a necessity.*

The main idea is 'shopping / is becoming / a leisure activity' – pattern (2): subject / verb / object.

Subjects and objects can consist of noun phrases: a head noun and more information about the head noun. In the sentence above, the head noun in the object is 'activity', and 'leisure' tells us what type of activity it is.

The following example is a longer sentence:

> *The growth of CCTV cameras, of the use of private security firms and of the blurring of public and private land has been an issue in cities such as Exeter.*

The main idea is 'the growth / has been / an issue' – pattern (3): subject / verb / complement.

We can find this structure quickly by looking for the verb first. We need to look for 'conjugated' verbs, i.e. verbs which tell you something about 'how many' or 'when', e.g. *drinks* (about the present, and referring to one person), *drank* (referring to the past), *are drinking* (about more than one person, referring to the present). Verb forms ending in -*ed* and -*ing* (i.e. participles) and *to*-forms are not conjugated verbs, but they can be part of conjugated verbs (e.g. *is drinking*, *has drunk*, *have lived*).

In the second sentence, 'blurring' is not a conjugated verb, but a gerund: a verb used as a noun. The main verb is 'has been': 'has' is a conjugated verb in the present perfect form that tells us that the subject is singular (referring to one person).

Once we have found the conjugated verb, it is easy to find the subject that corresponds to it. The subject in the second sentence is a very long noun phrase ('the growth of CCTV cameras, of the use of private security firms and of the blurring of public and private land'). The way to find the head noun, and to reduce the sentence to its basic form, is to say: 'what or who + verb?' Here this would be 'What has been (an issue)?' The answer is 'growth'.

Exercise 1

Reduce these sentences to their basic parts. What is the basic sentence pattern in these sentences? The first one has been done for you.

1 The demand for labour has fallen in almost all the periods of structural and economic change. *the demand / has fallen / in the periods: pattern 4*

2 A regulator gene controls the activity of an operator gene by the production of a repressor substance or of an inactive substance taking part in regulation.

3 The treatment of the difficulties of means testing and designing targeting mechanisms is discussed in O'Connor (2012).

4 The evidence on the effect of employment schemes on women in the developing economies in these regions is not conclusive.

5 Trade brings mutual benefits to all countries.

All the sentences in the exercise were simple clauses (groups of words containing a verb), i.e. they were not combined with other clauses.

Let's look at some examples of possible clause combinations.

In the following example, the clauses are equally important, so they are combined with a coordinating word. This word is 'but', which expresses contrast:

> *Trade brings benefits to all countries, but to some more than to others.*

Notice how in sentences like these, information is sometimes left out, because there is no need to repeat it:

> *Trade brings benefits to all countries, but (trade brings benefits) to some (countries) more than to others.*

Notice also how the two clauses could stand on their own, i.e. they are grammatically complete sentences:

> *Trade brings benefits to all countries.*
>
> *Trade brings benefits to some countries more than to others.*

Here is another example of coordinating clauses:

> *The previous evidence was not conclusive and the current data also show a mixed result.*

The two independent clauses are:

- the previous evidence was not conclusive

- the current data also show a mixed result

The coordinating word here is 'and', which expresses addition. Another common coordinating word is 'or', which links alternatives.

In the following examples, one clause is more important than the other, which is indicated by the type of word that is used to link them. The clause which is less important, the subordinate clause, gives background information. When you are reading your sources, be aware of subordination, as this will help you to see what is important and to follow the author's argument.

The following are examples of subordinating words:

- *that, what, who, whom, which, whose* (these introduce relative clauses and are often used in clauses that have a noun or adjective function)

- *when, since, after, while, because, so that, although, even, whereas, while, if, unless, provided that, assuming that, in order that, if ... then* (these are subordinators that are often used in clauses with an adverbial function)

Let's look at some example sentences:

> *Some towns are supported by campaigns which were started by residents who are concerned for the future viability of their town centre.*

If we try to reduce this sentence to its basic pattern, we can see that there are three conjugated verbs: 'are supported', 'were started' and 'are concerned'. However, the words 'which' and 'who' tell us that the information that follows is less important information. The most important information in the sentence therefore is:

towns / are supported (by campaigns)

- 'which' refers back to campaigns; the additional information is that they were started by residents

- 'who' refers back to residents; the additional information is that they were concerned

> *When the current of air creates a pressure which distorts the diaphragm, air pressure can be detected, which allows the speed of the air current to be determined.*

The conjugated verbs are 'creates', 'distorts', 'can be detected' and 'allows', but the most important part of the sentence is 'pressure can be detected' – the other verbs are part of subordinating clauses. The first one 'when the current ... diaphragm, ...' expresses a condition, and the second 'which allows ... determined' gives more information about the whole situation (that air pressure can be detected under certain circumstances).

The second example shows that it would be quicker to separate the sentence into clauses, before looking for conjugated verbs.

Being aware of what is important or not according to an author can enhance your reading comprehension and help you to paraphrase correctly, staying true to the point that the author wanted to make.

Use the following techniques to understand complex academic sentences:

- If there is only one conjugated verb, break the simple sentence down into its main components (head nouns, verb).

- If there are two conjugated verbs or more, find the most important clause (i.e. ignore the sub-clauses), and break this down into its main components.

- Start building the sentences back up: what extra information is there around the head nouns, what background information is provided in the sub-clauses?

In your analysis, be aware that there may be omissions, and think about what pronouns refer to.

Exercise 2

Analyse sentences 2–4 using the technique outlined above. The first one has been done for you.

1 Mass is directly proportional to volume for solids and liquids, so that the ratio mass/volume is constant on any observation, which shows the relationship between mass and volume.

- *mass / is / (directly)* **proportional** *(to volume) (for solids and liquids) [main clause]*

  [extra information: consequence]

- *the ratio (mass/volume) is constant (on any observation) [sub-clause]*

  [extra information: 'is constant']

- *this shows something (the relationship between mass and volume)*

2 Found in bony fish, a swim bladder is a bladder which is situated in the roof of the abdominal cavity.

3 Notation is a method of recording music, which is based on naming the notes by letters and also includes ways of distinguishing the value of notes in terms of duration.

4 Traditional models of urban zones, such as the models by Burgess (1920s) or Hoyt (1930s), place the Central Business District (CBD) in the middle of the town, which is unsurprising.

Possible difficulties

Some words have the same noun and verb forms, which can lead to confusion. Read the following sentences, in which the highlighted words have the same noun and verb forms:

1 The problem of consistency of the maximum position estimates has been treated in the literature by several authors.

2 Examination of the collected data for concentration measurements in public water supplies shows more than 20,000 positive readings.

3 The biomass increases of this type of macro fauna are harder to measure.

4 A mathematical expression has been developed to relate the field contrast with other data related to the surface.

Did you have to read them more than once? Sometimes our first interpretation is wrong. For example, in sentence 1, you may have read 'estimates' as a verb, but it is a noun in the subject.

Exercise 3

Are the words in bold in sentences 2–4 nouns or verbs?

Sentences that **contain reduced relative clauses** can also cause some confusion. Read the following sentence and decide whether it is correct and finished.

> *The organizations support the patients' meetings and clinics by providing printed information about heart disease and support available.*

Did you think that the ending was wrong, e.g. that it should say 'available support', or that it should continue (e.g. 'support available medical staff')?

The sentence was in fact correct. The underlying meaning is '... by providing printed information about heart disease and [about] support [that is] available.' In a reduced relative clause, the relative pronoun and verb are left out.

Analysing noun phrases

Noun phrases are commonly used in academic writing. We have already discussed that they can occur in the subject or object of sentences. In Chapter 5 we also mentioned that it is important that you can identify the head noun in your own phrases, to make sure that your subject and verb agree. Identifying head nouns is also important for your reading comprehension.

When you are reading, you may have to work out the meaning of new words, so it is important that you are aware of the different relationships between the nouns in noun combinations.

Glossary

blues N-PLURAL
If you have got
the blues, you
feel depressed.

charity (charities)
N-COUNT
A charity is an
organization
which raises
money in order
to help people
who are ill,
disabled, or very
poor.

fatigue
N-UNCOUNT
Fatigue in metal
or wood is a
weakness in it
that is caused
by repeated
stress. Fatigue
can cause the
metal or wood to
break.

Look at the following examples, which all give examples of restaurants:

1   Fast food restaurant

2   Neighbourhood restaurant

3   Palace restaurant

In the first example, a fast food restaurant sells fast food, it is all <u>about</u> fast food. The relationship between the nouns is *topic*.

The second example is different: the restaurant doesn't sell 'neighbourhood food', it is <u>in</u> the neighbourhood, and also <u>for</u> the neighbourhood. The relationship expressed by the nouns is *location* and *purpose*.

The last example is different again: the restaurant is not related to a place, it is not serving food to a palace, or based in a palace. 'Palace' is the *name* of the restaurant.

Topic, purpose, location and name are only some of the relationships between nouns. A few other ones are: material (*sea spray* – the spray consists of sea water); possessor (*student debt* – the debt belongs to the student); time (*winter blues* – the blues happen in winter); agent, i.e. the person who does something (*charity campaign* – the campaign is organized by the charity); characteristic (*metal fatigue* – the weakness is a characteristic of the metal); subtype (*plant cell* – a plant cell is a type of cell). Notice how the first or the second noun can express the relationship, e.g. in 'winter blues', the first noun 'winter' expresses the time relationship; in 'metal fatigue', the second noun' fatigue' expresses the characteristic.

When you have three nouns, you need to think about how all the nouns relate to each other, e.g. 'heart rate monitor' can be divided up as follows: 'heart rate / monitor': it is a monitor that measures heart rate, not a 'rate monitor' for the heart.

Exercise 4

Match the noun combinations with the relationships they express.

For example: 1 university policy – c topic : the policy is about the university

1	university policy	a	location
2	summer term	b	purpose
3	customer complaint	c	topic
4	customer receipt	d	name
5	university library	e	material
6	toothpaste	f	possessor
7	almond paste	g	time
8	Bernouilli principle	h	agent

The same issue occurs with adjective and noun combinations. In the example 'chopped Moroccan herbs', you need to work out that 'Moroccan' is an adjective not the noun referring to a Moroccan person: the herbs are Moroccan and chopped, and no Moroccans were chopped. Moroccan and herbs go together: this is about 'chopped / Moroccan herbs', not 'chopped Moroccan / herbs'. If you are buying 'dry cat food', you are getting cat food that is dry, not food for dry cats. Both 'dry' and 'cat' function as adjectives in front of 'cat'.

Thinking about which words go together in sentences can help you make sense of texts.

Exercise 5

Insert a line (/) to indicate which words go together.

1   university concert hall

2   post-traumatic stress symptoms

3   knowledge management systems

4   solid waste management

5   data stream systems

6   social science issues

7   human resource management

8   economic growth theory

Identifying signposts

It is normally not difficult to find the underlying general structure of a source, e.g. in articles and books, titles and subheadings are used to steer you in the right direction. Within the different parts, you may find a three-part-structure: introduction, main part and conclusion.

For more information on three-part structure and signposting, see Chapter 2.

You may find signpost words such as 'in conclusion' which clearly show you the function of the section that you are reading, but this is not always the case. The following sentences have been taken from an academic source. They are the first sentences of the different parts of the text (which can be identified by paragraphing and subtitles). Notice how they follow a pattern from the general to the more specific, and how they give clues about the rest of the section.

For the past 150 years, the increasing inequality of incomes has been a clear trend in the global economy.	general introduction of the topic
Two case studies, developed for this report, will illustrate the likely future employment trends.	clear indication of a two-part structure in the following text
In industrial countries the problem is relatively recent.	one area – raises the expectation that other areas will also be looked at
Although governments have to work within national constraints, the choices they make can help increase national incomes.	conclusion – this starts to answer part of the question the student was asked, about the role of governments in creating employment and incomes

If you do not understand a section of the source text, look for clues in the language to see how the section fits into the overall argument.

For example, in the following section, you should be able to find the **point**, the **evidence** and the **explanation**.

Tanzania has been recognized internationally for its success in Economic Empowerment of Women.	first sentence: **point**
The Global Gender Gap Report 2006 ranked Tanzania number 1 in terms of women's economic participation (World Economic Forum, 2006). The World Bank (2007) cites the National Bureau of Statistics (2002) in stating that women have been playing an important role in Tanzania's economy, especially in the agricultural sector where women make up 82% of the labour force. Overall, the 80.7% participation rate of Tanzania's women in the labour force is slightly higher than that of the men's rate of 79.6%.	following sentences: **evidence**
This suggests that the government's efforts to achieve gender equality have been successful.	last sentence: **explanation**

Another clue is the presence of counter-argumentation – as we saw in Chapter 6, this often precedes an author's actual claim.

Here are some examples of contextual clues that indicate counter-argumentation and other arguments presented by others:

Indicating counter-argumentation

One study has emphasized the need for ...

So far there has been limited agreement only on ...

Some studies have challenged this concept.

There is continuing debate about the value of ...

The literature shows some contradictory findings in this area.

For more information on argumentation and counter-argumentation, see Chapter 6.

It can be worth looking for the following patterns to enhance your understanding:

- the background, e.g. previous research

- the position of the author: which previous research they agree / do not agree with

- the claims that the author makes

- the evidence that is offered for each claim

- the comments that are made about each claim and/or evidence.

Claims the author makes

There are several drawbacks ...

There is not enough reliable evidence that ...

These are the most dangerous substances ...

One of the most significant patterns is ...

For more information on claims the author makes, see Chapters 8 and 10.

If you can identify what the function of a particular section is, you will be able to understand the individual points better.

Remember

✓ To really understand your source material, you need to use a combination of general and detailed analysis.

✓ A detailed analysis can be useful for a section that is difficult or that you may want to paraphrase.

✓ You can use your knowledge of sentence structure to break down the section into smaller components that are easier to understand, before putting it all together again.

✓ To avoid misinterpretations, bear in mind that some nouns and verbs have the same form, that words might be left out in relative clauses, and that noun phrases may need careful analysis.

✓ For the more general analysis, look for structural signposts that tell you the function of the section of text you are reading.

✓ Look for an argumentational pattern to see how the section fits into the overall argument the author is making.

8 | Authority

Quiz
Self-evaluation

For each statement below, circle the word which is true for you.

1	When writing an essay, I put all the information I have found together first, and then draw a conclusion from it.	agree | disagree | not sure
2	I know how to use cautious language to state my opinion.	agree | disagree | not sure
3	I know how to use personal pronouns appropriately to show my position on a subject.	agree | disagree | not sure
4	I can evaluate my own arguments to see if evidence needs to be provided and if it is strong enough.	agree | disagree | not sure

The principle of Authority

A question that students frequently ask is how an essay can be personal, when they are supposed to read similar sources and answer the same question as other students, and write in an impersonal style. In this chapter and the next we will look at how writers create their own identity in their writing.

The easiest way to answer the above question is that no two essays are ever the same. Two students may have used similar sources, and may write about the same solutions to a problem, stating the same evidence. However, they may still receive different grades. Here are some examples of what makes each essay unique:

- the exact sources that have been used

- the way the sources have been presented, e.g. the order in which they are used, the information that has been selected from them, how

Glossary

balanced ADJ
A balanced report, book, or other document takes into account all the different opinions on something and presents information in a fair and reasonable way.

the essay writer has related them to each other, the strength of the arguments, how the writer has explained the arguments, whether different opinions have been included to give a balanced view, which arguments have been relied on most, and which ones have been emphasized

- the language that the writer uses to organize and present views

- the essay writer's opinions and reasoning.

Developing a clear point of view

Glossary

preliminary ADJ
Preliminary activities or discussions take place at the beginning of an event, often as a form of preparation.

A student who has written an essay with a clearly developed point of view, which has been argued well through the use of sources, and who has made connections between the sources throughout, will receive a better grade than a student who has provided a list of the opinions of others without much comment on them.

It would be wrong to gather a lot of information, put it together and then draw a conclusion from it. To speak with authority, you should do the exact opposite: **form an opinion, based on preliminary reading if need be, and then use sources to justify it.**

Let's have a look at two examples taken from pre-university essays. The students were asked to think about car usage and consider whether private car ownership is still justified in the modern world or cars should be banned. Two students worked together and came up with advantages and disadvantages of cars, and put them in a table. They then wrote their short essays individually. Which essay just lists opinions, and which speaks with more authority?

Advantages of cars
popular: ownership keeps increasing convenient: they can get you from door to door, always available used by individuals and by businesses
Disadvantages of cars
damage to environment: pollution from manufacturing process, from driving cars and road building, petrol (oil) will run out cost: price of new car, cost of repairs, rising petrol prices risks to human health: more people die in car accidents than other transport accidents, increase in asthma and other illnesses traffic problems: too many cars, traffic jams cause delays and stress

Essay A

Cars have been debated for many years. Some say that they are convenient, whereas other people say that they are expensive, and cause problems for traffic, human beings and the environment. As they cause so many problems, governments should ban cars.

Many people have cars because they are available when and where they want them. If they want to go and visit family in a different city, they can just take their car and drive to the right address. If they took a train, they would still need to get to the station, and the train might not stop close to the address they want. Trains and buses do not travel at night, so they would not be able to visit family at certain times. Businesses also rely on road transport. Cars give people convenience, so they don't usually mind that they are expensive to buy and maintain (repairs and petrol) because it is worth it for them.

However, convenience is the only advantage that cars offer, and there are many disadvantages. Firstly, people die because of cars. More people die on the road than in other types of accidents and many are children on their way to school. People also die in road rage incidents when people get angry with other drivers for driving badly. They could also die or suffer from the pollution that cars cause, e.g. asthma is increasing.

Secondly, pollution causes damage to the environment. Most cars still use petrol, which causes damage. Moreover, building cars and motorways is bad for the environment too.

Lastly, these problems are going to increase because there are too many cars already and ownership will keep increasing. Having more cars also means more traffic jams, which will have a negative influence on business if they make business people miss appointments.

In conclusion, the disadvantages outweigh the advantages, so cars should be banned.

312 words

Essay B

Since their invention in the late 19th century, people have owned and enjoyed driving cars. This has caused well-publicized problems both for society as a whole and for individuals, yet car ownership is still on the increase. Although banning the car would solve many problems, the popularity of the car suggests that this is not a practical option.

In theory, people should be in favour of banning cars. There would be fewer deaths on the roads, fewer incidents of road rage, and a reduction in illnesses such as asthma and stress-related conditions caused by traffic delays. Apart from human health, the natural environment would also improve. First of all, pollution would decrease, as there would be fewer cars being manufactured and driven, and the network of roads would no longer need to be expanded. We would also have less need for oil, which is not a renewable resource. These are all benefits for society and for individuals. On a more personal basis, people would also save money, as they would no longer have to pay for cars themselves or be responsible for car-related costs such as insurance, repairs and fuel.

However, despite the fact that banning cars would protect the environment and save lives and money, it has never been part of any political agenda. There are probably a number of reasons for this, but the main issue is that cars have become too much a part of our lives. We can rely on them whenever we like to do business, travel and socialize. For over a century we have developed emotional connections with these machines, putting our personal convenience before the needs of society. When the large majority of people do this, personal preference becomes public preference, and change becomes impossible. We should not try to ban cars, but perhaps we should have banned cars while we still could.

310 words

Writing

Glossary

authoritative ADJ
Someone or
something that
is authoritative
has a lot of
knowledge of
a particular
subject.

Although students A and B use similar arguments, based on the same research, they have worked in very different ways.

Student A has put the arguments in favour and against next to each other and because there are more arguments against, she has concluded that cars should be banned.

Student B developed an opinion first. He personally would not want to ban cars, and thought this through: most of his friends had the same opinion, and political parties also don't suggest banning cars. He decided to argue against banning cars, but would have to find ways to explain why. He decided that the reason why nobody seems to want to ban cars had to be emotional attachment, as the rational arguments do not seem to convince anyone. He also thought that the reasons might be historical, because we have had cars for so long and also that perhaps the majority of people put their own interests and comfort first.

Whereas student A was merely listing the arguments, student B's essay is stronger because it focuses more on reasons. You need to have an idea and then use your evidence to support it (as in essay B), rather than put the evidence you have found together and draw a conclusion (as in essay A). Student B was using a thought process which is closer to what is expected at university.

Note that both essays should have included references to sources. In the next chapter, we will look at essay A again for this reason.

To show your reader where you stand on a subject, you need to distinguish your opinions from those of others. By using appropriate evidence from the work of published authors to develop your own arguments, and acknowledging the sources you have used correctly, you make your own views more convincing and make your own identity stronger in your essay. This makes your writing more authoritative.

For more information on how to correctly include and acknowledge the ideas of others in your work, see Chapter 9.

Stating your opinion: cautious language

Look at this example from a student essay:

> The implementation of anti-discrimination actions with long-term effects is therefore forgotten when managers have to deal with other urgent issues, such as new competitors.

The word 'forgotten' is probably too strong (and imprecise) here. Better choices would be 'delayed' or 'put on hold'.

We have already mentioned cautious language in the context of academic modesty. By using the language of possibility (rather than certainty), scholars acknowledge that their views are not the only ones, that they are open to being challenged, and that they respect other opinions and research. Remember that toning down a statement does not make it weaker, but more persuasive, and therefore academically stronger.

Here are some examples. Compare the two versions before you read on.

1   *Psychologists and anthropologists tend to have a different interpretation of what is realistic.*

2   *Psychologists and anthropologists have a different interpretation of what is realistic.*

Sentence 2 is a generalization, which readers may feel is too strong and they could easily say that it is incorrect. Sentence 1 says there is a pattern ('tend to'), not a fact, so it does not claim this is always true. Readers will be more easily persuaded about the truth of this statement.

There is another reason for cautious language: sometimes it indicates that we are reading the writer's interpretation or opinion, as in the following example:

> *The ratings were 4 or 5 for every aspect of the course. This is normally interpreted as evidence that the students are very satisfied with the course. However, here the relatively fast speed of completion and the lack of differentiation, i.e. the absence of ratings of 1 and 2 <u>may</u> also be an indication that the students did not take the questionnaire seriously enough.*

Notice how the cautious language is used to comment on data: 'normally interpreted' is contrasted with what happened here, which the writer thinks 'may be an indication' of something completely different.

In the following example, the writer is using cautious language to draw conclusions and make recommendations:

> *In other words, this method of PR <u>is likely</u> to be more effective and the company <u>could</u> benefit from using it to avert future crises.*

For more information on cautious language, see Chapter 4.

The use of 'I' and 'we'

Glossary

stance (stances)
N-COUNT
Your stance on a particular matter is your attitude to it.

intent (intents)
N-VAR
If you state your intent in a piece of writing, you say what you intend to do in the writing.

In Chapter 4 we discussed that it is good to avoid 'I' and 'we' where possible, mainly because of academic modesty, but that sometimes they are appropriate. The use of these personal pronouns is also linked to identity, so we need to look at them again. Here we will concentrate on how they, and other personal pronouns, are used by writers to show their stance.

Personal pronouns such as *I, we, my* and *our* are used in several ways to bring the writer and their identity into the text, which is appropriate in certain contexts. As can be seen in the following examples, they are used to:

- make personal views clear: *My concern is …*

- contrast the writer's approach with other people's methods: *My definition … is based on Munson's but combines this with …*

- write about the personal actions of the writer (e.g. research, experiments): *Experiments have been carried out by Nelson and Smith (1993) and Ojha and Mazumder (2008). In our experiment …*

- refer to people in general, 'all of us': *We know that … has consequences … that are still apparent … today …*

- relate the reader to the writer: *As we have seen, …*

They are also used to organize the essay, state its intent, and distinguish between the opinions of the writer and those of others, as shown in the following examples.

Glossary

scandal
(scandals)
N-COUNT
A scandal is
a situation or
event that is
thought to be
shocking and
immoral and
that everyone
knows about.

In the first example below, the student has been asked to look at the way the media has reported on a particular British political scandal of her choice and the people involved. Compare the two versions before reading on.

> 1 *In this essay the 'cash for honours' scandal was chosen, because it was the first time that a prime minister was interviewed by police investigating corruption. First, the background of the scandal will be given, followed by the way the different media reacted, especially to the involvement of the prime minister, Tony Blair.*
>
> 2 *I have chosen to discuss the 'cash for honours' scandal, because it was the first time that a prime minister was interviewed by police investigating corruption. I will give the background of the scandal and an account of the way the different media reacted, with a particular focus on the involvement of the prime minister, Tony Blair.*

The first example is not wrong, but it sounds strange. When reading the passive construction 'was chosen', the reader may wonder who chose it. Also, in this introduction to the essay, the writer is telling the reader what will come next. At this point, it is natural to refer to the person who has done this organization and use 'I'.

The following example is also from an introduction, where the writer states his intent.

> 1 *In this essay I argue that the worth of humanities as a subject of study cannot be measured just by economic considerations.*
>
> 2 *This essay argues that the worth of humanities as a subject of study cannot be measured just by economic considerations.*

Both versions are acceptable, but note that the use of 'I' in the first sentence makes the identity of the writer stronger. This works well here as it emphasizes the value of the research, perhaps in contrast with the views of others (who measure economic considerations only).

For more information on showing your stance in writing, see Chapter 10.

Evaluating your own arguments

To make your essay stand out, you have to show your point of view in the ways that we have discussed above. However, even if you express yourself clearly and explicitly and are using the right language, you will only speak with authority if your arguments are strong. You should evaluate your arguments in the same way as you look at those of others by considering whether evidence needs to be provided and if it is strong enough.

Exercise 1

Read the following short pre-university essay, which lacks authority because of problems with the arguments. Answer the question.

Which of the following can you find in this essay? They should all be avoided in essays because they are not academic ways of arguing. The first one has been done for you.

1   bias: looking only at the evidence that confirms your belief
    This essay is biased because it does not consider the evidence against the writer's opinion.

2   subjectivity: making claims without evidence, using negative or stereotypical (lacking originality) language

3   personalization or anecdotal (containing anecdotes rather than research) evidence: using a personal example ('this happened to me so this is what happens to everyone')

4   using absolutes (*no one, ever, all ...*)

5   attacking the person who makes the argument rather than arguing against what they say

6   being in favour of/against an argument because a lot of people are in favour/against

7   being in favour of/against an argument because an important person is in favour/against

8   misrepresenting a view so that it is easier to reject it

9   saying that something is true because there is no evidence that it is false

Because of the spread of the world's economic crisis, more and more people are asking for a single world currency system. Therefore, it is a good idea to implement this.

First, the risks involved in foreign exchange would no longer exist if we had a single world currency. In international trade, enterprises always face exchange rate risks. The loss caused by the floating exchange heavily counteracts their profit. Sometimes trading loss occurs in a very short time.

Second, it would be very convenient if we had a single world currency: people would not need to exchange money or pay service charges in the future. Everybody wants convenience above everything else when they travel, so one currency is better.

Last but not least, the competitive power of enterprises would improve if the prices for the goods and services were in same currency. It would be beneficial to social development.

Some say that it would be difficult to manage the currency, but these are the usual pessimistic economists. Given the evidence above, I still think that a single world currency should be put into practice in the future.

Tip ✓ Use the above list to help you evaluate the arguments in your essay.

Remember

✓ Your essays will receive a good grade if you don't just refer to different sources, but also comment on them and make connections between them.

✓ You can make your writing more authoritative if you select sources to develop your own argument rather than just list the information you have found about your topic.

✓ Using ideas from published authors to support your own arguments makes your writing stronger, not weaker.

✓ Equally, expressing your ideas cautiously, by talking about what is possible rather than what is certain, will make them stronger.

✓ Personal pronouns can be used to indicate a personal point of view, perhaps in contrast with that of others; and to distinguish between activities of the writer and others.

✓ Certain ways of arguing are not acceptable (e.g. showing bias, using personalization) and you will need to provide solid evidence.

9 | Integrity

Aims ✓ acknowledge the ideas of others   ✓ use citing and referencing techniques
✓ know when to cite   ✓ understand plagiarism better
✓ know whether to quote or paraphrase   ✓ avoid plagiarism

Quiz
Self-evaluation

For each statement below, circle the word which is true for you.

1	I know what citing and referencing are and why they are important.	agree | disagree | not sure
2	I know the difference between information that is common knowledge and information that needs a citation.	agree | disagree | not sure
3	I know the difference between a quote and a paraphrase.	agree | disagree | not sure
4	I know when to quote and when to paraphrase.	agree | disagree | not sure
5	I am aware of the reasons why plagiarism needs to be avoided and of techniques to avoid it.	agree | disagree | not sure
6	I feel confident about using citation formats.	agree | disagree | not sure

The academic principle of Integrity

Glossary

integrity
N-UNCOUNT
If you have integrity in academic writing, you are honest about what is your point of view and what is the point of view of other people.

In Chapter 8 we discussed the principle of Authority and considered how important it is to distinguish your opinions from those of others.

The other academic principle that applies here is Integrity, which is about honesty. By distinguishing between your point of view and that of others and referring to the sources you have used correctly, your writing will also demonstrate Integrity, as you are being honest about the extent of your own contributions.

First of all, we will look at the ways in which sources used in academic writing are acknowledged.

Citing and referencing

Citing is mentioning a source in your essay, such as an article or book, especially as an example or proof of what you are saying. It is an academic convention that the ideas of others are treated as intellectual property: they are owned by the people who expressed them first in that way.

Citing can be done through quoting or paraphrasing. **Quoting** is repeating what someone has said in exactly the same words, whereas **paraphrasing** is expressing what someone has said in a different way. Quotes are put between quotation marks.

When you quote, you need to give the name of the author, the year and the page number, e.g.

> *Wood (2011: 23) describes their textile industry as "flourishing", yet some analysts are indicating that it is in decline.*

When you paraphrase, you don't need to give the page number, just the name of the author and the year, e.g.

> *Whereas Wood (2011) has a positive view of the current state of their textile industry, some analysts are indicating that it is in decline.*

Referencing refers to the list of references you have to provide at the end of the essay, i.e. the details of the sources that have been used. One of the reasons for doing this is that your readers could then easily find the sources to read them too.

Acknowledging the ideas of others

Glossary

synthesis
(syntheses)
N-COUNT
A synthesis of different ideas or styles is a mixture or combination of these ideas or styles.

Your essay reflects your opinion throughout, except where you indicate that you are giving the views of others. This is why there is no need to use language such as 'I think' or 'I know'. However, essays also rely on common knowledge, and this does not have to be cited.

Your essay will be a combination of common knowledge, the original thoughts of others (cited), and your own unique synthesis and interpretation.

Writing

Glossary

reference work
(reference works) N-COUNT
A reference work is a book, journal, or article that you look at when you need specific information or facts about a subject.

verify
(verifies, verifying, verified) VERB
If you verify something, you check that it is true by careful examination or investigation.

It can be difficult to know whether you can assume that something is common knowledge, i.e. does not reflect a particular person's ideas, or whether you need to cite it. Here are some guidelines and examples:

Some types of common knowledge (no need to cite)	
a general fact that most people know	Aristotle and Plato were Greek philosophers who ...
a scientific fact that most people know or has been accepted for a long time	Every water molecule is made up of two units of the element hydrogen and one unit of the element oxygen.
a subject-specific fact that has been known or accepted for a long time	97% of the water covering the Earth is salt water found in the oceans.
a commonly used term or concept in your discipline	The meniscus, a small piece of cartilage that acts as a cushion in the knee joint, ...
information that can easily be found in general reference works	Advertising is a profession in which information about commercial products or services is produced.
a well-known quote from a famous source	Einstein said that $e=mc^2$.

You will need to cite in the following situations:

- when you would not have been aware of the information without a source (e.g. you actually used a general reference work to verify your information)

- when others are unlikely to accept what you say without evidence from a source

- when you have used a source in which the author presented common knowledge in a more personal way, e.g. by interpreting it differently; by adding an interesting insight; by presenting the information in an unusual format or order, or with a different approach; by phrasing it in an original or controversial way.

Tip ✓ Get into the habit of thinking critically about whether something is common knowledge or not. If a statement is not common knowledge, it will need a citation.

Exercise 1

Which of the following would you provide a citation for?

1   History refers to events from the past.

2   History refers to the collection and organization of information that relates to past events.

3   History is a record or account, often chronological in approach, of past events, developments, etc.

4   History is the version of past events that people have decided to agree upon.

5   History is an account, mostly false, of events, mostly unimportant, which are brought about by rulers, mostly knaves, and soldiers, mostly fools.

Exercise 2

Which of the following would you provide a citation for?

1   There are three states of matter: gases, liquids and solids.

2   Plaque, a substance containing bacteria, can be removed from the teeth by brushing and flossing.

3   Ice melts at 0°C.

4   Ice does not melt at 0°C.

5   Advertising is any paid form of non-personal presentation and promotion of ideas, goods and services through mass media such as newspapers, magazines, television or radio by an identified sponsor.

6   Advertising is just manipulation.

7   Galileo did experiments with balls of different sizes and weights.

8   Galileo was a man who was either loved or hated.

Tips   ✓ It can be a good idea to work with others to find sources and think about ideas.

✓ However, you need to think about the principle of Integrity: unless you are told to work on a group assignment, you should develop the ideas further on your own and write independently.

✓ Remember also that letting somebody copy your work is just as bad as copying theirs.

Exercise 3

Reread essay A from Chapter 8 below and indicate where sources need to be mentioned.

Essay A

Cars have been debated for many years. Some say that they are convenient, whereas other people say that they are expensive, and cause problems for traffic, human beings and the environment. As they cause so many problems, governments should ban cars.

Many people have cars because they are available when and where they want them. If they want to go and visit family in a different city, they can just take their car and drive to the right address. If they took a train, they would still need to get to the station, and the train might not stop close to the address they want. Trains and buses do not travel at night, so they would not be able to visit family at certain times. Businesses also rely on road transport. Cars give people convenience, so they don't usually mind that they are expensive to buy and maintain (repairs and petrol) because it is worth it for them.

However, convenience is the only advantage that cars offer, and there are many disadvantages. Firstly, people die because of cars. More people die on the road than in other types of accidents and many are children on their way to school. People also die in road rage incidents when people get angry with other drivers for driving badly. They could also die or suffer from the pollution that cars cause, e.g. asthma is increasing.

Secondly, pollution causes damage to the environment. Most cars still use petrol, which causes damage. Moreover, building cars and motorways is bad for the environment too.

Lastly, these problems are going to increase because there are too many cars already and ownership will keep increasing. Having more cars also means more traffic jams, which will have a negative influence on business if they make business people miss appointments.

In conclusion, the disadvantages outweigh the advantages, so cars should be banned.

312 words

Tip ✓ Providing a citation where one is not needed is fine, but not providing one where you should is wrong. If you are not sure whether or not a citation is needed, it is better to add one anyway rather than risk presenting someone else's work as your own by mistake.

Quote or paraphrase?

Paraphrases allow you to demonstrate more academic skills and are valued more highly. Half of your essay could consist of paraphrases.

Quotes are not as common in academic writing so you should not quote often. However, there are occasions when it is better to quote, e.g. when you want to include in your essay definitions, strong statements or ideas that were expressed by others in an original or authoritative way.

For more information on paraphrasing, see Chapter 10.

Tip ✓ When you want to present the ideas of others, paraphrase, unless there is a good reason to quote.

Exercise 4

If you were using the following information in your essay, would you quote or paraphrase it?

1　History is written by the winners.

2　Pop culture and fashion have been influenced for many years by Eastern culture. In part, this is due to the flourishing textile industry in countries such as China, Pakistan and India. Additionally, fashion has been inspired by colours and patterns that are prevalent in the East, with many Western designers including them in their ranges.

3　Fashion is a form of ugliness so intolerable that we have to alter it every six months.

Avoiding plagiarism

Glossary

invalidation
N-UNCOUNT The invalidation of someone's academic qualifications is a declaration that they are no longer valid.

expulsion
(expulsions)
N-VAR
Expulsion is when someone is forced to leave a school, university, or organization.

accountable ADJ
If you are accountable to someone for something that you do, you are responsible for it and must be prepared to justify your actions to that person.

Plagiarism can be described as academic theft, where scholars use the ideas of others without saying so. This can happen accidentally, e.g. where a student put the source in his list of references but forgot to indicate in the text where he used it, or it can happen deliberately, where ideas have been copied because a student did not want to do the work.

Accidental plagiarism can happen because of a lack of proofreading, so it is important that you leave yourself enough time to check your work. It can also occur because of lack of experience of the academic context, e.g. if in your school essays nobody minded if you included a few ideas in your work without saying where they came from.

Deliberate plagiarism can be caused by a lack of confidence, e.g. where the writer feels they can never be as good as the authors whose ideas and words he or she used. An extreme example of plagiarism is when somebody pays for an essay by somebody else, but even a few unacknowledged words in a text of your own can be plagiarism.

Some students may be unfamiliar at first with the stricter rules about the use of sources in English-medium universities, and the ways in which they have to be acknowledged.

However, there is no excuse for plagiarism. There is a reason why we've used the word 'theft' to describe it: it can be regarded as an academic 'crime'. The punishment ranges from reducing an assignment grade, to the invalidation of credits and degrees and expulsion from university.

Tutors tend to be very good at finding plagiarized sections, through a combination of having knowledge of the ideas and sources that are being used and of noticing a change of style between the plagiarized part of the text and the personal.

See if you can spot it yourself. Look at the following two sections from a piece of writing. One of them has a change of style in it; can you tell which one?

> 1 *Lastly, companies are accountable and need to ensure that all investors have access to clear and accurate information, because it informs them of the performance of the company within the market and will enable them to make the right investment decisions. All the principles mentioned above are critical for a company to develop corporate governance, but no enterprise can develop without the*

> *support of society and the natural resources of the environment. Therefore, in the next section, we will pay attention to the relationship between the company and society and discuss corporate social responsibility.*

> 2 *Successful companies with increasing sales need to make a decision about expansion, e.g. whether they want to produce more and hire staff. This means that the profit from the extra production and sales needs to be sufficient to cover the extra salaries and companies may not be prepared to take this risk. But if the competitors have paid attention to their lessons in economics, they will know that growth and increased production could bring their costs down, and therefore increase profit per unit. What do they know that you don't know? It's called economies of scale.*

You may have noticed that in section 2, the style is quite academic to start with, but towards the end it becomes more informal. Additionally, the beginning of the section talks about 'companies', whereas the end talks about 'you' and the competitors. The reason for this is that some of the information at the end comes from a website giving business advice. As we saw in earlier chapters, the style of any piece of writing is determined by its writer in response to the intended readers' expectations. Anything lifted from other sources will have a tone that is determined by the other writers and their intended readers, which makes plagiarism easy to identify. Another clear sign of plagiarism is when the student's writing is not as good as the published author's writing, except in the plagiarized sections.

Glossary

tone N-SING
The tone of a speech or piece of writing is its style and the opinions or ideas expressed in it.

Tip ✓ Never worry about not sounding as good as the original source. You are not meant to. Tutors prefer original work with some mistakes in it to plagiarized copies.

Exercise 5

The following example shows accidental plagiarism. Can you find it?

> *For instance, some explicit regulations and rules like after-sales taxes repayment are commanded by supervisors and managers. Finally, contractual agreements are said to range from the 'explicit' (formalized by printed contracts establishing legal bonds) to the 'implicit' (the rules based on social behaviours).*

Plagiarism is not just about academic integrity (and authority), it is also connected to the principle of academic accuracy. If you do not follow the referencing rules exactly (e.g. mentioning every author, providing page numbers for quotes, following conventions in your reference list), then this can be considered (accidental) plagiarism.

Tips When you have finished the essay, proofread in two directions:
- ✓ Check that all the authors that are mentioned in the essay are mentioned in the reference list.
- ✓ Check that all the names in the reference list have been mentioned in the essay itself.

Just a few reasons to avoid plagiarism

- It is a form of theft.

- It is cheating, so it is wrong.

- You are wasting your time as you are not learning how to write like a scholar or developing your knowledge.

- You are wasting your tutor's time as they are not reading / giving feedback on your work.

- It makes your grade worthless, so you won't be able to feel proud of your work.

- It is easily detectable and leads to serious consequences.

- You will spend a lot of time worrying about being detected.

- If it does remain undetected, it hurts others because of unfairness, and yourself, because you will always know your grade is meaningless.

Other types of plagiarism

You need to be aware that plagiarism is more than accidental or deliberate theft. It can also occur where a quote or paraphrase has been made up, or the ideas from the original text have been changed, perhaps to provide more evidence for the point that a student wants to make. As deliberately misrepresenting a writer's words is also considered plagiarism, you need to take care not to do this accidentally: always make sure you understand the original text. If you cannot completely understand it, then do not try to paraphrase it.

Another type of plagiarism occurs when students submit the same piece of writing twice, i.e. to get credit again for the same work. If you think that some of the writing you have done previously, e.g. for another tutor in another year, may be relevant for a new assignment, then quote or paraphrase yourself as you would any other author.

Another issue to look out for in order to avoid plagiarizing is that your paraphrases do not contain too much text that is identical to the original text. You are supposed to use your own words to convey the ideas from the original text.

Following citation guidelines

There are different citation systems; your university will make it clear which one you are supposed to use. Examples are Harvard, Vancouver, Chicago, APA and MLA. Different departments within a university may have different guidelines, e.g. law students may be asked to use the OSCOLA system (Oxford Standard for the Citation of Legal Authorities), theology students may be asked to use footnotes for religious text quotations, though most other departments discourage footnotes. Usually, you will be trained on how to use citation systems and/or given detailed guidelines.

There is citation software available, but this is normally only used by those who have to write very long academic texts, such as theses. Note that even if you use software, you will need to be aware of citation principles.

Citation conventions are important and you will need to pay attention to every detail, such as knowing where full stops go.

In the exercises below, Harvard referencing is being used. There are different versions of Harvard, so instead of following the one below in your essays, you should always check which system you are required to use. Use the exercises to practise following guidelines and proofreading for detail. Developing these skills will help you with any other citation systems.

Citation formats

When quoting or paraphrasing, the name of the author and the year of publication of the source can be given after the source information, between brackets. The author's name can also be used as the subject of the sentence. Here is an overview of the two possibilities for quotes and paraphrases:

	Quote	Paraphrase
1 **Author as subject of the clause**	Wood (2011, p. 82) describes their textile industry as 'flourishing', yet some analysts are indicating that it is in decline, e.g. (...)	Whereas Wood (2011) has a positive view of the current state of their textile industry, some analysts are indicating that it is in decline, e.g. (...)
2 **Author mentioned after the citation**	Their textile industry has been described as 'flourishing' (Wood, 2011, p. 82), yet some analysts are indicating that it is in decline, e.g. (...)	There have been positive evaluations of their textile industry (e.g. Wood, 2011), but some analysts are indicating that it is in decline, e.g. (...)

Note that page numbers are given for quotes, but not for paraphrases.

So far we have seen examples from books and articles written by one author, but it gets more complicated than that. In the exercises on pages 111 and 113 you will find some guidelines that cover more examples of in-text references.

Exercise 6

Read each guideline and correct example in the boxes. Is the example underneath correct according to the rules?

1

Source	Article or book by one author
Example	*There has been a tendency to emphasize the individual differences in the student learning experience (e.g. Kinginger, 2008).*

Correct example?

The value of formal instruction has also been investigated in this context (e.g. Huebner, 1995).

2

Source	Two authors have written a book or article together
Example	*However, these test scores only provide limited information (Collentine and Freed, 2004).*

Correct example?

However, numerous communicative opportunities are assumed to be obtained from 'a variety of out-of-class environments in which students find themselves while living in-country' (Brecht and Robinson, 1995, p. 317).

3

Source	Three or more authors have written a book or article together
Example	*This also applies to previous research in this field (e.g. Brecht et al., 1995).*

Correct example?

Other research (e.g. Lapkin et al, 1995) investigated general proficiency.

4

Source	An official publication with no named author
Example	*The Criminal Defence System helps ensure that the Criminal Justice System is both fair and efficient (Legal Services Commission, 2004).*

Correct example?

The size and profits of P&G cannot be matched by any other packaged goods company (P&G Annual Report, 2012).

5

Source	The author has published more than one article or book in one year
Example	*Not only do the needs of patients need to be taken into account in these circumstances (Freeman, 2011a), health services need to be able to show evidence of this (Freeman, 2011b).*

Correct example?

These insights are not new (Ngole, 2013A).

Note that the abbreviation of the Latin 'et alii', which means 'and others' is used in the text. In the reference list all the authors need to be named.

The list below is a reference list based on some of the sources mentioned above. Here the information on the left is added to show how different sources need different referencing styles.

The following are always included: **author surname, author initial, date, title, place of publication, publisher.**

Notice where page numbers have been included, e.g. for chapters in books and articles in journals. Page numbers are always included where available or appropriate.

The reference list has to be alphabetical, based on the first mentioned author, as in the first two examples below. It is normally on a separate page, not indented, and with a line space between each source.

Chapter in a book	Brecht, R., Davidson, D. and Ginsberg, R., 1995. Predictors of foreign language gains during study abroad. In *Second language acquisition in a study abroad context*, ed. B. Freed, pp. 37–66. Amsterdam: Benjamins.
Chapter in a book	Brecht, R. and Robinson, J., 1995. On the value of formal instruction in study abroad: student reactions in context. In *Second language acquisition in a study abroad context*, ed. B. Freed, pp. 317–333. Amsterdam: Benjamins.
Journal article	Collentine, J. and Freed, B., 2004. Learning context and its effects on second language acquisition. *Studies in Second Language Learning*, **26**, 153–171.
Chapter in a book	Huebner, T., 1995. The effect of overseas language programs: report on a case study of an intensive Japanese course. In *Second language acquisition in a study abroad context*, ed. B. Freed, pp. 171–191. Amsterdam: Benjamins.
Journal article	Kinginger, C., 2008. Language learning in study abroad: case histories of Americans in France. *Modern Language Journal*, **92**, 1–124.
Online newspaper	Liang, L., 2012. Study abroad and broaden your mind. *The Guardian* [online], 16 August. Available from: http://www.guardian.co.uk/education/2012/aug/16/clearing-studying-abroad [accessed 12.08.12].

Exercise 7

A student included the following sources. Have they been referenced correctly?

Journal article	Rivers, W., 1998. Is being there enough? The effects of homestay placements on language gain during study abroad. *Foreign Language Annals*, **31**, 492–500.
Chapter in a book	Lapkin, S., Hart, D. and Swain, M., 1995. A Canadian interprovincial exchange: evaluating the linguistic impact of a three-month stay in Quebec. In *Second language acquisition in a study abroad context*, ed. B. Freed, pp. 67–94. Amsterdam: Benjamins.

Following citation and referencing guidelines will allow you to indicate clearly which comments are yours, which ideas have been borrowed from elsewhere, and where these ideas can be found. This will make your essay more authentic and help you to avoid accidental plagiarism.

Remember

✓ If you are not sure whether an idea is common knowledge or not, cite it, just in case.

✓ You should paraphrase rather than quote where possible.

✓ There are many reasons why plagiarism is wrong and the penalties can be severe.

✓ There is no excuse for plagiarism, not even accidental plagiarism. Make sure you present the source text accurately, and acknowledge clearly and carefully where it came from.

✓ You can also avoid plagiarism by following citation guidelines carefully.

10 | Paraphrasing

Aims ✓ use a technique to paraphrase accurately ✓ integrate paraphrases grammatically
✓ use paraphrases to show own opinion ✓ use paraphrases to summarize

Aims

? Quiz
Self-evaluation

For each statement below, circle the word which is true for you.

1	I know how to paraphrase correctly.	agree | disagree | not sure
2	I know how to integrate paraphrases in my writing to show my opinion about the ideas in the paraphrase.	agree | disagree | not sure
3	I know whether to use present or past tenses when paraphrasing.	agree | disagree | not sure
4	I know a variety of verbs that I can use to introduce the ideas of others.	agree | disagree | not sure
5	I know the difference in meaning between the verbs I use to introduce the ideas of others.	agree | disagree | not sure
6	I know how to bring together the work of different authors in my paraphrases.	agree | disagree | not sure

Paraphrasing technique

In the previous chapter we looked at how important it is to acknowledge the ideas of others and how to do this. In this chapter we will concentrate more on how to integrate these ideas into your own text. We will examine how your choice of tenses and verbs affects meaning, but first we look at a paraphrasing technique that will ensure that your paraphrases are relevant, accurate, original and integrated.

A useful paraphrasing technique is the following one, which consists of six steps.

1 Decide how the ideas from the original text **fit** into your essay (you do not need to use all the details from the section of the text that you are looking at, only the relevant ones).

2 **Read** the original piece of text **repeatedly**, until you really understand its meaning.

3 Put the original text **away**.

4 Write down in **note** form, and in your own words, what the text says.

5 **Compare** your notes with the original:

   a have you expressed the same meaning?

   b have you used your own words?

6 **Integrate** the information into your text so that your essay clarifies it and builds on it; use grammatical **sentences** that link the information to the text around it.

Note that this technique works in exactly the same way if you are using a source in another language: you should not translate literally.

An easy way to remember the six steps, until you have paraphrased so often that you remember them anyway, is to use the acronym 'FRANCIS':

1 <u>F</u>it?

2 <u>R</u>ead (Repeatedly)

3 <u>A</u>way

4 <u>N</u>ote (own words)

5 <u>C</u>ompare

6 <u>I</u>ntegrate <u>S</u>entences

FRANCIS will help you!

Glossary

integrate
(integrates, integrating, integrated) VERB
If you integrate one thing with another, or one thing integrates with another, the two things become closely linked or form part of a whole idea or system. You can also say that two things integrate.

acronym
(acronyms)
N-COUNT
An acronym is a word composed of the first letters of the words in a phrase, especially when this is used as a name. An example of an acronym is NATO which is made up of the first letters of the 'North Atlantic Treaty Organization'.

Paraphrasing is not about substituting words for other words and changing the word order of the original sentence. Doing this can lead to too much of the original text being reproduced, which can constitute plagiarism. Apart from these problems, you may also end up with a paraphrase that simply doesn't work. Consider the following example.

Original source:

Dealing with housing problems was considered the greatest priority.

Paraphrase:

✗ *The main concern was believed to be taking action on accommodation trouble.*

This paraphrase does not sound natural and does not make sense. Instead, you could use the FRANCIS technique explained above. Assuming that this idea Fits in (F) with the points you are writing about, you would Read (R) and reread the sentence until you really understand it. Visualization could help here. Then, when you put the text away (A), you could end up with the following notes (N):

housing problems / first

When Comparing (C) with the original text, you would notice that 'housing problems' is exactly the same phrase as in the original, but that you did manage to note the main ideas.

Putting the ideas in your own words, in a way that Integrates the Sentences (I S) in your text, you may get:

The housing situation needed to be improved first.

At this point you would compare with the original again to check that you have represented it well. Here it was important that you used a past tense.

You may end up using synonyms and different word forms, changing actives into passives (and the other way around) and changing the word order of the original, but as a result of your understanding of the whole idea, not as a technique to 'hide' the original text.

In Exercise 1, you will practise step 5, comparing (C).

Exercise 1

Step 5: comparing. Look at the following three paraphrases and compare them with the original text. Do they express the same meanings and have the writers used their own words? Which is the best one?

> **Original text**
>
> Pop culture and fashion have been influenced for many years by Eastern culture. In part, this is due to the flourishing textile industry in countries such as China, Pakistan and India. Additionally, fashion has been inspired by colours and patterns that are prevalent in the East, with many Western designers including them in their ranges. [taken from a book by Wood, published in 2011]
>
> **Paraphrase 1**
>
> *China, Pakistan and India have had a great influence on the West. One example is their textile industry, which is growing and therefore influencing fashion and popular culture. Western designers are also using colours and patterns that influence the East (Wood, 2011).*
>
> **Paraphrase 2**
>
> *Western fashion is familiar with Eastern culture, for example, typical Eastern colours and patterns have often been used in fashion designs. One reason for this is the success of the Eastern textile industry (Wood, 2011).*
>
> **Paraphrase 3**
>
> *Clothing trends and popular culture have been affected for a long time by the culture from the East. The Chinese, Pakistani and Indian clothing industries are thriving, which can partly explain this influence. Moreover, stylists from the West have added Eastern colours and designs to their collections, which shows how the fashion industry has been influenced (Wood, 2011).*

The importance of integration

Quotations or paraphrases can never stand on their own – they always need to be linked to the sentences around them.

The following examples show two extremes. Paraphrase 1 shows no evidence of how it relates to the surrounding text. Paraphrase 2 supports what the writer is saying in the surrounding text. (The paraphrases are in bold.)

Writing

Glossary

anatomically
ADV
If the body of
a person or
an animal is
anatomically
large, it is
physically or
structurally
large.

The original text

Researchers have taken brain scans that show that anatomically, dolphins have relatively large brains, similar in some aspects to those of highly intelligent beings such as humans. [taken from a text by Burns, 2010]

Paraphrases

1
Dolphins are much researched animals. **Burns (2010) says that dolphins have been scanned and it demonstrates that physically their brains have similarities to human brains and are big for their body size.** This makes them very interesting animals.

2
Dolphins have always been considered reasonably intelligent, based on the fact that humans could teach them tricks. **There is now scientific evidence that dolphin brains show similarities to human brains and are large for their body size (Burns, 2010).** If dolphins are even more intelligent than previously thought, this raises questions about the way they are treated.

The writer of paraphrase 2 demonstrates that she has understood the text by Burns, by fitting it in well into the point she is making about the intelligence and treatment of dolphins. In the first paraphrase, the writer only demonstrates that she has read the text by Burns, and that she can change the words and the order of the information. She has not demonstrated her understanding, as the other sentences just make general comments ('much researched', 'very interesting').

Step 6 (Integrate Sentences) is very important. As we said, paraphrases are not language exercises in which you change some words. Instead they are representations of the ideas of others, and should be integrated in a way that shows that the original source is understood and how it relates to the new idea that is being developed. To do this, introduce the paraphrases clearly (think about how they fit in with your essay) and comment on their meaning afterwards (think about what they mean), whenever possible.

In the following example from a student essay, you can see how the student has integrated the paraphrases (in bold) well. The student first of all pointed out the contrast between low compliance and the efforts that were made ('Despite …') and showed in this way that she understood the source text. The second paraphrase, introduced by 'They have also claimed that' is linked to the previous one and seems to introduce a slight change in topic, which will probably be developed further in the essay.

> Despite all the efforts that are made by the NHS and all the studies that address the importance of such methods in controlling infections, Magiorakos et al. (2010) pointed out that compliance of healthcare providers is still very low, and that even if it reaches a reasonably high rate it will be difficult to sustain this. They have also claimed that there are other factors associated with poor hand hygiene compliance.

In Exercise 2, you will practise step 6, integrating sentences (IS).

Exercise 2

Step 6: integrate sentences. The text below is the paragraph that comes before the paraphrase. Which of the two paraphrases underneath would <u>integrate</u> well after the paragraph?

The fashion industry has recently been influenced by the increased global interest in what Africa as a continent can offer us. The catwalks have been showing block prints, feathers, beads and bright colours. One possible reason for this interest is the state of the global economy: people feel a need to surround themselves with cheerful colours and accessories in difficult economic times. Designers have also become more socially responsible, which has resulted in stronger links with ethical African brands and projects that ensure fair labour and sustainable employment in poverty-stricken areas.

Paraphrase 1

Also, Western fashion is familiar with Eastern culture as its typical Eastern colours and patterns have often been used in fashion designs. One reason for this is the success of the Eastern textile industry (Wood, 2011).

Paraphrase 2

The East has been a more long-term trend in fashion, with typical Eastern colours and patterns often being used in fashion designs. One reason for this is the success of the Eastern textile industry in countries such as China, India and Pakistan (Wood, 2011).

Exercise 3

Look at part of an essay below and note where the writer wants to add a paraphrase. Then follow the six steps (FRANCIS) to decide which part of the original text is useful and to paraphrase it correctly.

The essay

Some scientists have suggested that dolphins are so intelligent that they should be treated as a person, albeit a non-human one. [paraphrase to come here] This raises questions about how dolphins are being treated now.

The original text

It has long been known that chimpanzees are bright animals, and with their human-like appearance and their ability to learn, they have been considered similar to people. Now scientists are saying that dolphins communicate in ways that are similar to human communication and that they are brighter than chimpanzees, which are considered by some to be as intelligent as three-year-old children. Researchers have taken brain scans that show that anatomically, dolphins have relatively large brains, similar in some aspects to those of highly intelligent beings such as humans. Perhaps surprisingly, the researchers have been able to establish that dolphins are able to think about the future. They can learn, and pass their newly-learnt skills on to others.

[written by Burns, 2010]

When you are integrating your paraphrase into your essay, it is also important to remember to make it clear where a paraphrase ends and where you continue with your own ideas. For example, in the text below, the student needed to put 'They have also claimed' in the last sentence. Without this indication that she was still paraphrasing, the idea in the last sentence would be considered her own.

> Despite all the efforts that are made by the NHS and all the studies that address the importance of such methods in controlling infections, Magiorakos et al. (2010) pointed out that compliance of healthcare providers is still very low, and that even if it reaches a reasonably high rate it will be difficult to sustain this. They have also claimed that there are other factors associated with poor hand hygiene compliance.

Showing where your point of view fits in

neutral
ADJ-GRADED
If someone uses neutral language, they choose words which do not indicate that they approve or disapprove of something.

PR N-UNCOUNT
PR is an abbreviation for public relations. Public relations is the part of an organization's work that is concerned with obtaining the public's approval for what it does.

When referring to the ideas of others, writers can show that they agree, disagree or are neutral about them. Let's have a look at how a student writer develops some of his points in an essay about public relations in times of crisis for a company.

> *On the other hand, if companies can deal with social networking, they may be able to handle the crisis well (Veil, Buehner and Palenchar, 2011).*

The writer has chosen to paraphrase what he read and has integrated the research in his argument ('on the other hand'). By choosing to paraphrase this research in an integrated way, the student is saying that it is relevant for his topic and he agrees with it. He is using the source to persuade the reader that he is making a valid point.

The following example is from an essay about feminist research. Notice how the student develops her ideas: she gives two reasons why more women entered the workforce, one of which is based on a source. The text has been shortened; this is indicated with (…).

> *There have been a considerable number of women in the workforce for decades. During and after World War II there was a sharp decrease in the number of men; hence, women had to do men's work in the factories. (…) Additionally, due to the process of globalization, the international labour force has experienced a dramatic change in its composition, particularly in terms of demographic, age and gender (Cassell, 2006).*

In the following extract, the student's point is given in the last sentence: that it is important that companies communicate quickly in times of crisis. He bases this on two areas of research, mentioned in the previous sentences.

> *Researchers have shown that people found negative information more attention-grabbing than positive and that it is weighted more in forming the overall evaluation of the company (Fiske, 1980; Skowronski and Carlston, 1989). It also has been suggested that the way a company handles negative publicity is one of the most influential factors for consumers when they make purchase decisions (Advertising Age, 1995, cited in Ahluwalia et al., 2000). Therefore, it is important that during crisis communication PR people are able to minimize the potential damage and restore the company image and the brand as quickly as possible.*

The choice of verb can also show the student's stance. Reporting verbs (also called 'verbs of reference') such as 'point out' and 'claim' are important because the verb you choose tells the reader about your attitude to what you are reporting. In the following example, the student uses the verb 'point out', which indicates that she agrees with the research.

> *Coombs (1998) points out that when a company is perceived as being responsible for the crisis, accommodative strategies should be used, in order to emphasize image repair.*

The verb 'point out' is used to present facts, so if you say that an author pointed something out, you are saying that they stated a fact. If you use the verb 'claim', you are saying that what the author says may not be true, or is certainly not generally accepted. Similarly, if you think the author has argued something well, you may say that they have 'demonstrated' something, whereas if you are not persuaded by the argument, you might choose the verb 'argue'.

It is therefore very important that you understand the exact meaning of the verbs that are frequently used to report the research of others. Some students try to avoid repeating themselves by using these verbs as synonyms. However, they have different meanings. Although it is important to vary your language, it is more important to express yourself correctly.

For more information on showing your stance in your writing, see Chapter 8.

Exercise 4

Match the verbs with their meanings.

For example: 1 e; argue = state something and give the reasons why it is true

1	argue	a	tell others about something, draw their attention to it
2	assert	b	state that a theory or explanation is possibly or probably true, because it fits in with evidence
3	claim	c	state something that you believe to be true but without proof, so it may be false
4	indicate	d	state something firmly
5	point out	e	state something and give the reasons why it is true
6	propose	f	show that something is true or exists

Exercise 5

Match the verbs with their meanings.

For example: 1 f; acknowledge = accept or admit that something is true or that it exists

1	acknowledge	a	show by means of argument or evidence that something is true
2	allege	b	say that something (negative) is true but without proving it
3	demonstrate	c	say something which you believe to be true
4	imply	d	say something that is likely to be true, e.g. because it is a necessary consequence
5	prove	e	make something clear to others
6	suggest	f	accept or admit that something is true or that it exists

Exercise 6

Five of the 12 reporting verbs in Exercises 4 and 5 introduce facts, whereas the others present opinion, and mean that there is a possibility that people might disagree. Can you separate them? Write them under two headings: Presenting facts and Presenting opinion.

Presenting facts	Presenting opinion

Writing

Glossary

feminist empiricism
N-UNCOUNT
Feminist empiricism is the belief that people should rely on practical experience and experiments, rather than theories, as a basis for knowledge, and that these should not favour or be concerned with one gender more than the other.

dualist ADJ
If a person or their way of thinking is dualist, they believe that something has two main parts or aspects.

In the following extract, the writer stays neutral. She discusses different research positions and some of the criticism and support that these have received (see <u>underlined</u> sections), but does not indicate which position she finds most valuable.

> *Saratankos (2005) suggests that there are three main feminist research positions. Firstly, feminist empiricism is less radical. (…) The second position is the feminist standpoint, which suggests knowledge is based on experience (Harding, 1987). It is argued that women are in the best position to do research on women because women understand better about women than men; hence, women have unique opportunities to do research (Saratankos, 2005). (…) It is therefore <u>most accepted by feminists</u> as it is closest to the mainstream of feminist origin. Finally, feminist postmodernism is the more recent perspective which (…) refuses the usage of dualist groups of thoughts. It argues that there are different types of women in terms of age, occupation, sexual orientation and ethnicity; hence, different standpoints need to be adopted. Moreover, the world is viewed as endless stories or texts, for instance gender is constructed through language. <u>This position, therefore, criticizes traditional research and practices</u>.*

As she has not indicated what she agrees or disagrees with, the student's identity is not very strong in the extract above. However, in the next part of the essay she goes on to assess different research studies. Notice how the student manages to give her opinion very clearly and how it has been informed by the general criticism of the different research positions that were mentioned in the extract above.

> *Undoubtedly, the different findings from the studies above allow a better understanding of policies and practices regarding women in the workplace as well as the role of unions and management in addressing gender issues. However, the research studies have some drawbacks. They are all conducted by women; hence, it is difficult to be sure that the perspectives are unbiased. Moreover, the small samples from some workplaces cannot represent every organization as a whole. Additionally, these studies emphasize gender as the key debate but overlook the importance of other factors, such as age, race and ethnicity that shape the differences between women.*

In the next example, different sources are being contrasted. By doing this, the student has demonstrated that he understood their content.

> *Whereas Dean and Liff (2010) focus on the importance of three industrial relations actors, Foster and Harris (2005) emphasize the organizational context in which both managers and external environments influence diversity practices.*

We would expect the next sentence to continue explaining the point by Foster and Harris.

Exercise 7

Answer the following questions for the extract below.

- What is the writer's opinion?

- Does the writer agree with the sources he quotes?

- Do the different sources express the same idea, or are they separate components of the argument?

If the company is small, it could ignore equality actions by using 'word of mouth', which is indirect discrimination but much faster and cheaper (Dickens, 2005). Furthermore, the priority of any organization is profit (Noon, 2010). The implementation of anti-discrimination actions which have long-term effects is therefore forgotten when managers have to deal with other urgent issues.

Integrating quotes and paraphrases grammatically

Grammatically speaking, when we want to mention what somebody else has said, we can choose direct speech or indirect speech.

Direct speech – the exact words someone has said – is put in quotes:

> *Serrant-Green stated that there 'appear to be as many arguments for outsider research as against' (2008, p. 38).*

Note that the exact words that the author has used have to be put between quotation marks that indicate where they start and finish. The author's surname, the year of the source's publication and the page number on which the quote appears need to be mentioned.

If a quote is quite long, first of all ask yourself if it is wise to include the whole quote. If you decide to include a quote which covers four lines or more, then you need to set it apart visually. Your style guidelines will tell you how. For example, this could involve using an indented block quote, using a line spacing of 1 rather than 1.5, and not using quotation marks.

Exercise 8

Quotes need to be integrated grammatically into the new sentences. In the following sentences this is not the case. Make corrections.

1   Redmond (2003: 12) defined the low income groups as: 'Low income is defined as $725 or less.'

2   According to Grelling (2006: 98), to protect the construction materials of the bridge they used 'Chemical additives used in the concrete and waterproofing systems.'

3   Atkins (2010: 42) said that: 'Burj Al Arab, the world's most luxurious and tallest all-suite hotel in Dubai.'

Indirect speech, also referred to as reported speech (it reports what someone has said), is used where we make changes to the words that were originally written, which is why we find it in paraphrases.

> *Serrant-Green (2008) states that outsider research seems to have the same number of benefits as drawbacks.*

While choosing the appropriate verb of reference to show our opinion about what we are reporting, we also need to bear in mind that the choice of verb affects the grammatical pattern in the sentence. The 12 verbs from Exercises 4 and 5 above can all be followed by a clause, the pattern _that_ + *complete sentence*.

Some verbs are followed by a noun phrase:

They	discussed examined	the potential <u>problems</u> with this type of test.

Other verbs are followed by a different type of clause, the pattern _question word_ + *complete sentence*.

The authors	show report	how a variety of technologies is already being used to engage students more.

Some verbs can follow more than one pattern:

They	suggest show	that	these data could be interpreted in different ways.
		how	these data could be interpreted in different ways.
		a different <u>interpretation</u> of the data.	

There are some other patterns, e.g. infinitive and *-ing* forms can follow the verbs:

> *The interviewees claimed <u>to</u> have had some of the answers beforehand.*
>
> *They suggested limit<u>ing</u> the number of participants to 10.*

Tip ✓ Make sure that you know the patterns for the verbs you use regularly and pay attention to the patterns that are used in the articles or other types of research that you read.

Exercise 9

Match the sentence parts to make complete sentences. You can use each ending more than once and you don't need to use them all.

The authors ...

1	concluded	
2	argued	that all languages have them.
3	identified	them in all the languages in the sample.
4	claimed	how all languages have them.
5	implied	

Choosing the right tense

The general rules about tense choices apply to Academic English.
In the table below you can see what determines the choice of present, past, simple and perfect tenses.

	PRESENT	PAST
SIMPLE	■ Habit ■ General truth ■ Some specific contexts (e.g. newspaper reports, recipes)	■ Past action (specific time) ■ Past action (no longer true)
■ active	*study/studies*	*studied*
■ passive	*am/is/are studied*	*was/were studied*
PERFECT	■ An action began in the past and continues in the present ■ An action occurred in the past (time is not specified) ■ An action has occurred more than once in the past	■ An action was completed by a definite past time/ before another past action
■ active	*have/has studied*	*had studied*
■ passive	*have/has been studied*	*had been studied*

Let's look at some examples in an academic context.

If you write about what specific researchers did, rather than about the opinions or conclusions they reached, then you use the simple past:

Horwell and Baxter (2006) **investigated** *toxicity levels in small particles.*

If the focus is on the opinions that researchers hold, rather than the activities they undertook to reach them, you use the simple present:

Andrews (2010) **sees** *argumentation as a vital skill in Higher Education.*

If you are writing about research activity that spanned a period of time, e.g. because different authors worked on the same area, then the present perfect is more likely:

Many studies **have asserted** *that the increase in the incidence of inflammatory bowel diseases, asthma and allergic diseases in industrialized countries is mainly due to immature immune systems, insufficient exposure to microbes, intestinal microbial ecosystem imbalances and genetic inheritance disorders (Penders et al., 2010 and Pochard et al., 2002).*

When you are reporting on a study that was done in the past, you can present the results with a past or a present tense, depending on what you want to emphasize.

You can use the past tense if you are neutral about the outcome of the experiment. You simply present the information as something that was true in the past:

> *They showed that the toxicity levels **were** higher.*

If you want to keep some distance from the findings, e.g. because they were true only in those specific circumstances, you can also use the simple past:

> *Horwell and Baxter (2006) showed that fine particles (<1 μm), and ultra-fines (<0.01 μm), **were** likely to be the most toxic.*

If the information that is being presented is generally accepted as a fact then you use the present tense. You would also use it if you wanted to emphasize that the information is current or relevant, or if you wanted to show that you agree with it:

> *Horwell and Baxter (2006) showed that fine particles (<1 μm), and ultra-fines (<0.01 μm), **are** likely to be the most toxic.*

Notice that in the last two examples, the first verb 'showed' was in the simple past: the authors showed this in 2006. In the exercise below, pay attention to whether you need to decide on the tense of the reporting verb (such as 'show') or the verb that refers to the information that is being reported on.

Exercise 10

Choose the correct tense for the underlined verbs.

1   Bassaganya-Riera et al. (2012) **(a)** <u>report</u> that the commercial probiotic VSL#3, which contains Lactobacillus acidophilus, stimulates mucosal cellular immunity against colorectal cancer in mice, while the experiments done by Maroof et al. (2012) **(b)** <u>indicate</u> that the previous bacterium enhances systematic immune response against breast cancer in mice.

2   Studies done in Scottish hospitals <u>reveal</u> that one in five patients suffering from HCAI had been diagnosed with methacillin resistant Staphylococcus aureus (MRSA) infection (HPS, 2011).

3   Furthermore, the examined data **(a)** <u>show</u> that 236 patients **(b)** <u>are</u> between the age of 1 to 23 months and 467 patients were over 65 (NHS choices, 2012).

Summarizing

Glossary

further
(furthers,
furthering,
furthered) VERB
If you further
something,
you help it to
progress, to be
successful, or to
be achieved.

Summarizing is similar to paraphrasing, but rather than working with a small section of text which you use to further an idea in your essay, you put together ideas from different parts of a text, or from different texts (synthesizing). You also focus on the main ideas rather than on a particular one. This is what this would look like:

> 1   summary from different parts of the same source:
>
> *Cook (2006) emphasizes the individual differences in the student experience and supports the use of ethnographic data.*
>
> 2   synthesis from different texts:
>
> *There has been a tendency to emphasize the individual differences in the student learning experience (e.g. Churchill, 2006; Cook, 2006; Kinginger, 2008).*

Within the text, you can choose to put the authors' names alphabetically or chronologically.

Note that in the reference list, each author will need a separate entry, in alphabetical order.

As we have seen in this chapter, the choices you make about grammar and vocabulary are important when you are integrating the ideas of others. They affect the meaning you are trying to convey. Use FRANCIS to make sure that paraphrasing is an academic skill, not a language exercise.

Remember

✓ Paraphrases should be used to further the arguments that are being developed in the essay. This means they won't look like the original text any more, and will be integrated in the new text, but will still express the original idea.

✓ Make your paraphrases relevant, accurate and integrated by using FRANCIS.

✓ You should always explain the relevance of quotes or paraphrases in your text – don't include them without comment.

✓ Your choice of verb to introduce a quote or paraphrase can show whether you agree or disagree with the paraphrase.

11 | Essay process and presentation

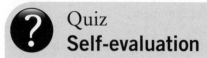

Aims ✓ the stages in the essay writing process ✓ presentation
✓ time management ✓ other types of academic writing

❓ Quiz
Self-evaluation

For each statement below, circle the word which is true for you.

1	I am aware of the steps involved in writing an essay.	agree | disagree | not sure
2	I often get distracted with emails, social networks and other messages when writing an essay.	agree | disagree | not sure
3	I often spend hours on end in front of the computer without breaks.	agree | disagree | not sure
4	I always check for common errors at final draft stage.	agree | disagree | not sure
5	I am aware of aspects of presentation such as font size, line spacing, paragraphing, etc.	agree | disagree | not sure
6	I am familiar with the content and format of reports, case studies and reflective writing.	agree | disagree | not sure

From essay question to meeting the deadline

In the previous chapters, we looked mainly at the principles and requirements of the academic essay genre, and at the kind of language you are supposed to use. We have considered what the final product of the essay writing process should <u>be</u> like (e.g. authoritative, conventional, modest). In this chapter we will consider in greater depth what it should <u>look</u> like, i.e. how it should be presented. We will also discuss the similarities and differences between essays and some other academic genres. First we will look at the essay completion process itself.

The writing process

When you wrote shorter essays, it may have been possible to sit down, think, plan, write and check in one go. Longer essays are very different in nature, because of:

- their length: more organization and signposting is required

- their research component / referencing conventions

- their increased levels of formality and sophistication of language.

As a longer essay is also more complex, the process leading to it is not straightforward. The following graphic, which is linear, is a simplification. In reality, you are likely to move back and forth between the stages, e.g. by updating your outline after doing some research or by reorganizing notes about a particular subject into a paragraph before continuing to take notes about other topics.

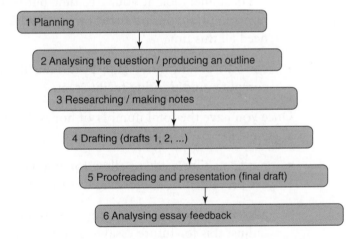

Figure 1 The six steps in the essay writing process

Planning

The amount of time you spend on a particular assignment will depend on a number of factors. If the assignment is worth a lot of marks, you are likely to put in a greater effort. The larger the word count, the more time it will take. Your previous knowledge of the topic, the availability of the sources, and the deadline all play a part. You can also decide how high you want your mark to be; if you are aiming higher than a pass, you will

Glossary

allocate
(allocates,
allocating,
allocated) VERB
If one item
or share of
something is
allocated to
a particular
person or for
a particular
purpose, it is
given to that
person or used
for that purpose.

want to spend more time and effort on the work. Your assignment could be your priority, or alternatively one of many equally important study tasks or something that competes with more important issues in your life.

For these reasons, it is impossible to say how much time you need to spend on essay preparation and writing. What you need to do is consider the above issues and plan so that you allow yourself enough time to do the work to the standard you want it to be.

If you have a lot of time, you may be tempted to work slowly, but then you might run out of time. Alternatively, if you feel the deadline is too soon, you might rush through certain stages or risk not allowing time for proofreading, which can have a very negative effect (see below).

Here is a practical way to manage your time. Look at your diary and do the following:

- work out the time you have available each day between now and the deadline: look at your free time but be realistic about how many hours in total you can focus on your work each day and whether you need all this time

- consider practicalities: transport time, library opening times, computer and printing facilities, etc.

Once you have the total number of hours that you can dedicate to the assignment:

- put some time aside to allow for emergencies (those times that you are prevented from working due to unforeseen circumstances)

- allocate half of the remaining time to research and half to the writing (adjust this for future essays as your experience will tell you which stages take you a long time, and you will probably write more quickly in the future); think about the first five stages.

Assuming you have some time each day, your plan could look like this:

50% Research time stages 1–3	50% Writing time stages 4–5	Reserve time
e.g. Tuesday–Friday week 1	e.g. Sunday–Wednesday week 2	e.g. Thursday–Friday week 2

NOW .... DEADLINE

Figure 2 Suggested time allocation

Be realistic and give yourself enough time spread over several days: overdoing it will lead to stress, which is counter-productive. You will also need to allow for plenty of breaks.

Tip ✓ Although planning is important, don't spend too much time on it or use it as a way to avoid starting to write.

Analysing the question / producing an outline

In Chapters 1 and 2 we covered most of what you need to know to effectively analyse a question and produce a useful outline. To help you plan your essay better you could also add approximate word counts to the different parts of the essay outline. Not only does this give you a better idea of what your final essay will look like, it will also help you plan stage 3, the research, as you will know how much information you are looking for on a particular topic.

Let's look at an example from an outline from Chapter 2 with added word counts for a 2,000-word essay:

Introduction	background about parallel trade, including definition	200 words
Main body	■ a description of each of the causes of parallel trade	400 words
	■ the aims of international marketers / an explanation of the different problems that parallel trade causes them	600 words
	■ the importance of these problems, with reasons	300 words
	■ possible solutions with examples	300 words
Conclusion	comments about how big the problem of parallel trade is for international marketers and if it can be successfully minimized	200 words

This also helps you avoid a common mistake which wastes a lot of your time: writing too many words. Some students really get into the writing process and then have to cut words or whole sections out of their essay, which is a shame because of the work that is wasted and the time that is lost. The skill with longer essays is to select only the most important information, i.e. what is necessary to develop your argument.

Researching / making notes

In the research stage, don't forget to:

■ note the bibliographic information of each source, without making mistakes: the author's surname and initials, the full title, the publisher, the year of publication, the place of publication, and the chapter or pages if applicable

■ make sure that the section is worth reading in detail before you spend more time on it

■ make notes while you are doing detailed reading, indicating clearly which are the words from the author and which are not

■ write down the exact words and page numbers for possible quotes

■ adapt the style of your notes to your purpose: choose the right visual representation, and use concise language (abbreviations, symbols, ...).

For more information on researching and making notes, see Chapter 6.

The first draft

Glossary

procrastination
N-UNCOUNT
Procrastination is when you keep leaving things you should do until later, often because you do not want to do them.

inspiration
N-UNCOUNT
Inspiration is a feeling of enthusiasm you get from someone or something, which gives you new and creative ideas.

Look at the first draft as a warm-up or practice activity before you do the real work. As is the case for competitive sports, warm-ups and practice help you with your performance, but nobody judges you on the preparatory work. It is especially important you do not judge **yourself** at this stage. If your standards are too high, you may be at risk of writer's block, an inability to start or to continue writing.

The causes of writer's block are:

- setting your standards too high

- expecting too much too soon

- thinking about what others expect from you

- comparing yourself to others or aspiring to an ideal

- self-doubt, fear and stress, which may lead to procrastination

- lack of motivation, possibly leading to distractions.

Other reasons are a real inability to do the work and lack of inspiration, but as you have got to this stage in your studies and are working from research notes, these should not apply in your case.

The following can help:

- remind yourself that this is the first stage, where there is no need for judgement

- replace thoughts of what others want with calming thoughts, e.g. of a beautiful landscape

- do nothing for a few minutes except breathing slowly, preferably with your eyes closed, as this can calm you down and clear your mind

- develop a writing ritual, e.g. always start to write after you sip some water or chew sugar-free gum while you write

- remove any distractions (internet, gadgets, books, ...)

- just start writing **anything**; sometimes you just need to start writing to get into it

- motivate yourself by reminding yourself that this assignment is a necessary part of your overall goal, and therefore you have chosen to do it

- set yourself a small achievable task and deadline to start, e.g. 'In the next ten minutes I will put together the three definitions of my topic and write two comments about how they compare.' Then set yourself another small task.

- say out loud what you want to write as it can help you to formulate your thoughts.

It is fine for your first draft to be full of spelling and grammatical mistakes, badly formulated sentences, words in your first language, etc. This draft is only a first attempt to move away from an outline and notes towards the development of your ideas.

The next drafts

After finishing your first draft, it is a good idea to leave your work until the next day at the earliest. You can then fill in gaps, reorder paragraphs, make clearer links and generally try to make sure that everything is logical and expressed clearly. This is the stage in which you should think about academic principles and appropriate language. Use your critical reading skills (see Chapter 7) on your own work to identify weaknesses in the argumentation. Through a continuous process of making changes and rereading, your essay versions will keep improving.

For more information on reading comprehension skills, see Chapter 7.

Tip ✓ Pay particular attention to the organization of your ideas. Are you starting from the general to the more specific and indicating with headings and topic sentences what you are trying to say? If there is clarity in these areas, the reader will not be too concerned about any language mistakes you may have made.

The final draft

Although nobody expects you to write a perfect essay, your reader will become irritated if you have not presented your content clearly and if:

- you still make basic mistakes (e.g. spelling), especially in subject-specific vocabulary

- you make mistakes that are easily avoidable (e.g. an unfinished word or sentence)

- you make too many mistakes.

If you give the impression that you do not care enough about your work, the reader may not want to spend too much time on it either, which is bound to have a negative impact on your grade.

If you have not already done so in previous drafts, look for common errors and the typical errors you are likely to make. For some students, this may be subject-verb agreement, for others it will be the difference between 'your' and 'you're'.

For more information on common errors, see Chapter 5.

Exercise 1

Find the mistakes in the following paragraph. Look only for spelling, subject-verb agreement, sentence construction, word forms, stating the obvious and missing words.

> In this essay I will be using resources such as textbooks, the internet and scientific journals in order to come to a conclusion about how forms of firm organization has changed by particularly focusing on three dominant models, which are proto-industrialization, factories and big business.
>
> The essay is divided into three main parts. Fistly, historical contexts and characteristics of each model are given. Secondly, the essay explores advantages as well disadvantages of each form. Particular models are looked at in terms of timeframe, location, important institutions that affect the choose of location, as well as examples of successful industries or businesses followed the model.
>
> Finally, a brief discussion is given to take into account factors that influence model application, which is followed by a conclusion.

Layout and presentation

The final draft is also the time when you need to think about presentation. You may already have done so previously, but there is no real need to do so until this point.

Look at any guidelines you were given by your tutors regarding font size, line spacing, paragraphing, title pages, etc.

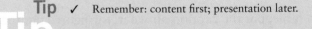

Tip ✓ Remember: content first; presentation later.

If you are left to make those decisions yourself, then the following guidelines will be helpful.

- Use a separate page for the title and your details (e.g. your name and/ or student number, the tutor's name, the course number, the deadline date).

- Number the pages that follow.

- Use subtitles for long essays (from 1,500 words upwards if it helps with clarity).

- Don't use bullet points or numbered lists.

- Leave enough space between the lines (e.g. 1.5) and generally allow enough white space, e.g. before and after visuals.

- Have wide margins (e.g. 2.5 cm on each side of the paper).

- Leave a line between each paragraph.

- Start each paragraph at the beginning of the line or indent five spaces; be consistent.

- Choose a classical font style and size, such as Times New Roman or Courier 12.

- Do not use colour or fun graphics (i.e. impress the reader with content only).

- Do not use underlining and bold except in headings.

- Do a spell check – choose 'English (United States)' or 'English (United Kingdom)' as appropriate.

- Use left justification.

- Do not use headers or footers.

- Start your reference list on a different page.

- Start every appendix (if you have any) on a different page.

- Put one space between each word, after every comma (,), semi-colon (;) and colon (:).

- If you use a table, put the caption above it, for figures put the information below. Number tables and figures separately.

Look at the essay at the back of the book to see what these guidelines make an essay look like.

Analysing essay feedback

You may be allowed to talk through a draft with a tutor for some essays, but usually the first time you will receive feedback is when it has been graded. It can be tempting to focus on the grade, especially if it is a good one, but the feedback you receive is full of useful information that you can use to inform your future essays. Do not skip this stage as it is essential if you want to keep improving throughout your studies.

For more information on analysing essay feedback, see Appendix 2.

Other types of writing

Glossary

objective ADJ
If someone is objective, they base their opinions on facts rather than on their personal feelings.

In this book we have mainly considered essays that are given as assignments. The same academic principles we have discussed also apply to essays written under exam conditions. The differences will be a reduction in:

- length

- number of sources used

- time for planning / thinking / writing.

Generally speaking, the main difference between essays and reports is structure. Again, the academic principles are the same, as reports will need to be clearly organized, written in an objective style, be accurate, be referenced, etc.

A report usually starts with a page which outlines the different headings and subheadings in the report, which are numbered (e.g. 1, 1.1, 1.2, 1.3, 2, 2.1, ...).

Reports are likely to be more descriptive than essays. A typical report will describe and comment on original research, e.g. an experiment or a survey. You may be told which format you have to use, or you could use the classic IMRAD pattern, which is common in scientific and engineering subjects, as follows:

- Introduction

- Methods (and Materials)

- Results

- (Analysis and) Discussion / Conclusion

Exercise 2

1 Put the following report contents under the right headings.

- description of the meaning and significance of the findings, e.g. whether they were expected or not
- design/procedure of survey/experiment
- how the information was gathered / the experiment was carried out
- limitation of methods, materials and other aspects
- outcome of the experiment/survey/comparison ...
- relevance of the problem
- suggestions for further reading
- summary of the project/research
- the background of the problem/project
- the purpose of the report/research
- relevant research about the topic

Introduction	Methods	Results	Discussion and conclusion
relevance of the problem	*design/procedure of survey/experiment*		

2 Which of these four parts is the main one?

Case study reports are pieces of writing that focus on a particular real-life issue.

Case studies are used in many different departments for a variety of reasons. In medicine, it could be a risk assessment; in political science it could be an analysis of the emergence of a social movement; in business, it could be an examination of the operational management of a particular company; in education it could look at the way technology is introduced in a particular teaching environment.

The difference between essays and case studies is not very clearly defined. The subject matter is the main difference, with a case study taking a detailed look at a practical example. Check with your department if they have any specific guidelines about what you are expected to cover in a case study.

To clarify what case studies are about, we will look at two examples of student work based around case studies.

- The first example is a case study which is part of an essay about Public Relations. The question was:

> *'Consider the potential use of both traditional and social media engagement for crisis communications. Use a case study approach, using a comparison between positive and negative examples, and make use of crisis communications theory in your analysis.'*

The student wrote up the case study in essay form. She chose to discuss the Domino's Pizza YouTube Crisis of 2009, which involved a prank video of two employees spoiling food about to be served. The student included a timeline of events and company reactions in table form:

Domino's Pizza YouTube Crisis

1 Timeline

Date	Company reactions

In the following section, entitled '2 Analysis', the student examined the company's reactions. She supported her argument by using paraphrases from relevant literature with in-text citation.

- In the second example, the student was given a text which described the history of a local company. He then had to analyse the company's current strengths and weaknesses and make marketing recommendations.

The student chose to write up the case study in report format. He used the following headings: background, data analysis, options, recommendations.

First, he provided a summary of the company's situation and raised the most important issues that he wanted to discuss. In the data analysis section he considered the company's strengths and weaknesses. He then considered possible actions that the business owner could take to address the company's weaknesses. In his recommendations he narrowed the solutions down to the most practical short-term and long-term options.

Because of the potential for different formats in a case study, you will need to follow your instructions carefully.

'Reflection' is 'careful thought about a particular subject'. Reflective pieces of writing, such as a diary entry, a reflective essay, or a personal development record, usually require you to react to a real-life experience by relating your thoughts, opinions and learning processes. Their general purpose is to demonstrate evidence of your learning.

In Medicine, you may be asked to write down your reflections about a placement, in Education you might be asked to comment on a class you have observed, in Social Sciences you might be asked to comment on an article you have read.

Although the focus will be on your personal observations and reflections, you may be asked to relate these to theories and research in your field. The following pattern may be a useful way to organize your writing, but always consider the specific instructions you have received:

- context (introduction)

- what you observed, what you did and how you did it

- evaluation (feelings about the events, possible explanations, theoretical connections)

- what you have learnt, ideas for the future, summary (conclusion).

Glossary

research report (research reports) NOUN A research report is a document that you write which shows the results of your research.

literature review (literature reviews) N-COUNT If you do a literature review, you read relevant literature such as books and journal articles so that you have a good, basic knowledge of a topic.

Bear in mind that your purpose is always academic and that your work will be read by a tutor. On the one hand, you will be able to use 'I' freely and describe what you did and thought (i.e. it is more personal), and use more non-academic vocabulary and grammar (more active verbs, words such as 'find out' rather than 'establish'). On the other hand, because of the academic environment of both the writer and the reader, there will still need to be formal elements, such as clear organization and presentation, careful proofreading, and language features such as using full forms (instead of contractions).

It can be difficult at first to understand the requirements of this mixed genre, so study examples from other students if possible.

Although essays are still the most common genre in many disciplines, the types of writing mentioned above – and many more – are also becoming more popular. What you are asked to write will depend very much on your discipline, e.g. an engineer could be asked to write a design specification, a literature student might write a critique, business students may do some collaborative writing. The purpose of these pieces of writing varies: sometimes you will have to demonstrate theoretical or practical knowledge, perhaps linked to your future professional field; at other times you will be asked to look back at your learning experiences. These purposes are linked to the stage you are at in your studies: at the beginning of your studies you might be asked to write lab reports but towards the end you may need to write a research report, which also includes a literature review. If you want to start a PhD you will be asked to write a proposal.

Some of these types of writing have clearly defined parts, others are more flexible.

It is impossible to cover all the different formats you might be asked to write. However, the guidelines below will help you think about the requirements of any genre:

- ask your tutor for guidelines

- ask for examples from previous students

- do a library or online search for examples

- examine previous examples by asking yourself the following questions:

  - who is the intended reader?

  - what does the intended reader want to find out?

  - what knowledge or skills do I need to demonstrate? (purpose)

  - what are the different parts (organization), what style is being used (level of formality), what is a normal length?

Exercise 3

Look at the following extracts. Notice the difference between the two pieces of academic writing. Ask yourself who the writers are and what the purposes of their pieces of writing are.

1 The original specification dimensions of the product were supposed to be 23 cm square with a tolerance of 5 mm. The final product measures 14 cm by 14 cm. Although the size of the final piece differs from the original specification, it has resulted in a better outcome. The change occurred due to constant development issues with the construction method, which after numerous failures resulted in the final piece being smaller and easier to carry. This change has made the product more compact and space efficient, with the circuits being spaced out enough so that they are easy to change and replace without the risk of damaging anything else.

2 Today's lecture was about microfinance (MF). I had already learnt about this on my previous course but I noticed there were some references to articles I did not know about and I made a note to read these. In the group discussion I thought everybody would agree about the value of MF schemes, but in our group two people started to have an argument. I felt that the whole group should have been included but it was hard to convince them to widen the issue or to finish talking about their particular issue.

Remember

✔ Reduce essay stress by making a time management plan and by following the tips to avoid writer's block.

✔ None of the stages in the essay writing process should be rushed. After planning, analysing and researching, leave enough time for drafting, re-drafting and proofreading.

✔ Don't underestimate the importance of presentation, but don't worry about it until the essay is written.

✔ Before starting to work on a new essay, look back at previous feedback to make sure you keep improving.

✔ When you are asked to write a different genre, use your essay writing skills but adapt your style and format.

Appendix 1 – Taking your writing up to the next level: Example essays

In the following section you will find two essays. The first one is a pre-university essay and the second one was written for a postgraduate course. We will take a close look at both essays, as a reminder of the academic conventions and principles that have been covered in this book, and with the aim of helping you to take your level of writing up to university standard. If possible, try to read essays in your discipline. Many university departments put examples online for their students.

Example essay 1

Look at the example 250-word essay below. You may have written similar essays before: it could have been written by a student preparing for an IELTS exam or a student preparing for end-of-school exams.

This particular essay was written by a student who wanted to enter an English-medium university. It was an effective essay: the student received a writing grade high enough to admit him onto a Master's course in engineering.

Comment and analysis

Strengths

Overall, we can say that the writer has argued well by making his points clear, with evidence and explanations where necessary. He has organized the writing into paragraphs and has used words such as 'firstly' to show the reader how the arguments in the essay relate to each other. He has used a variety of academic and subject-specific vocabulary and has demonstrated his ability to vary tenses, and to use impersonal constructions such as passives correctly. Read the positive comments below that relate to specific points in the essay.

> *In your opinion, what are the most serious urban transport problems we are currently facing? Identify possible solutions and say whose responsibility these are.*

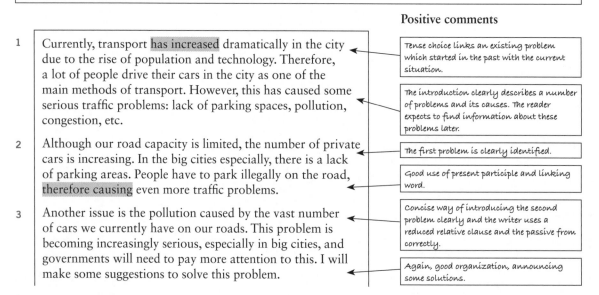

Positive comments

1   Currently, transport has increased dramatically in the city due to the rise of population and technology. Therefore, a lot of people drive their cars in the city as one of the main methods of transport. However, this has caused some serious traffic problems: lack of parking spaces, pollution, congestion, etc.

Tense choice links an existing problem which started in the past with the current situation.

The introduction clearly describes a number of problems and its causes. The reader expects to find information about these problems later.

2   Although our road capacity is limited, the number of private cars is increasing. In the big cities especially, there is a lack of parking areas. People have to park illegally on the road, therefore causing even more traffic problems.

The first problem is clearly identified.

Good use of present participle and linking word.

3   Another issue is the pollution caused by the vast number of cars we currently have on our roads. This problem is becoming increasingly serious, especially in big cities, and governments will need to pay more attention to this. I will make some suggestions to solve this problem.

Concise way of introducing the second problem clearly and the writer uses a reduced relative clause and the passive from correctly.

Again, good organization, announcing some solutions.

Appendix 1 – Taking your writing up to the next level: Example essays

Positive comments

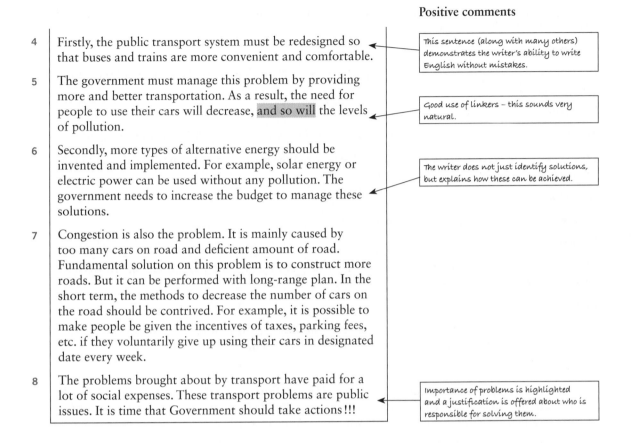

4   Firstly, the public transport system must be redesigned so that buses and trains are more convenient and comfortable.

> This sentence (along with many others) demonstrates the writer's ability to write English without mistakes.

5   The government must manage this problem by providing more and better transportation. As a result, the need for people to use their cars will decrease, and so will the levels of pollution.

> Good use of linkers – this sounds very natural.

6   Secondly, more types of alternative energy should be invented and implemented. For example, solar energy or electric power can be used without any pollution. The government needs to increase the budget to manage these solutions.

> The writer does not just identify solutions, but explains how these can be achieved.

7   Congestion is also the problem. It is mainly caused by too many cars on road and deficient amount of road. Fundamental solution on this problem is to construct more roads. But it can be performed with long-range plan. In the short term, the methods to decrease the number of cars on the road should be contrived. For example, it is possible to make people be given the incentives of taxes, parking fees, etc. if they voluntarily give up using their cars in designated date every week.

8   The problems brought about by transport have paid for a lot of social expenses. These transport problems are public issues. It is time that Government should take actions!!!

> Importance of problems is highlighted and a justification is offered about who is responsible for solving them.

Areas for development

Many of the characteristics of this piece of writing are not acceptable at university. The style is not academic enough: there are clichés, repetitions, imprecise expressions, informal words and punctuation marks. Look at the numbered paragraphs in the essay and the corresponding comments below.

With regard to organization, the introduction and conclusion could be much stronger and the transition between the ideas in the main body is often confusing. There are some incorrect word choices, and there are also grammatical mistakes, e.g. regarding prepositions and articles.

Issues like these can often be found in the writing of students who can already write quite well but are not used to the new system at university. Most of the problems with writing in the first year at university can be attributed to a lack of awareness of academic conventions and the extra demands for longer, more academic essays, with a different reader, purpose and type of content.

Paragraph 1

Currently, transport has increased dramatically in the city … Word choice mistake. 'Recently' would be better as it matches the tense choice which links a problem that started in the recent past with a current situation.

due to the rise of population and development of technology … Preposition mistake. It should be … *the rise in population*

Therefore, a lot of people drive their cars in the city as one of the main methods of transport. Linking word error. The fact that people use the car as a main method of transport is not a direct consequence of the development of technology. No linking word needed here.

lack of parking spaces, pollution, congestion etc. Use of 'etc' is inappropriate in an academic essay. It shows a lack of precision in your writing.

Paragraph 2

In the big cities especially, there is a lack of parking areas. Word choice mistake – 'big' is a little informal and unacademic.

Paragraph 3

This problem is becoming increasingly serious, especially in big cities. Repetitive use of vocabulary.

I will make some suggestions to solve this problem. Avoid the use of *I* in academic essays, except in those circumstances described in Chapter 8, page 96.

Paragraph 4

No need to separate paragraph 5 from paragraph 4.

Paragraph 5

The government must manage this problem by providing more and better transportation. Incorrect referencing device. It's unclear what *this* refers to here.

Paragraph 6

Secondly, more types of alternative energy should be invented … Word choice mistake. As energy is a naturally occurring resource, it is rarely invented – 'sourced' would be better here.

Paragraph 7

Congestion is also the problem. Incorrect article use. *The problem* suggests there is only one problem, whereas the essay describes many. *and deficient amount of road* … Word choice mistake. … *and a poor road network* is better. *Deficient* doesn't collocate with *road*. Also, an article is needed before *poor*.

Fundamental solution on this problem … article needed. *A fundamental solution*… Preposition mistake. … *to this problem* …

But it can be performed with long-range plan … Wrong word choices. Suggest *But this can only be achieved as part of a long-term plan* …

the methods to decrease the number of cars on the road should be contrived … No article needed. Instead of *contrived*, which has negative connotations, *created* or *invented* would work.

For example, it is possible to make people be given the incentives of taxes, parking fees … Passive form not needed. Suggest: *For example, it is possible to incentivize people by reducing their taxes* …

Paragraph 8

It is time that Government *should take actions!!!* Exclamation marks are not normally used in academic writing.

Appendix 1 – Taking your writing up to the next level: Example essays

Example essay 2

The following essay was the first one written by an international student studying for an MSc in HRM (Human Resource Management). She received a merit for it.

Study it, paying particular attention to organization, citations, register and style, academic principles, and other topics that have been covered in this book. There are some comments, both positive and negative, to guide you.

When you have read Example essay 2, go back and compare it with Example essay 1. You will see that the difference between them is not just about word length and subject matter: the second essay demonstrates a much higher awareness of the academic genre.

Why are equality and diversity in the workforce so difficult to achieve? Why have attempts to enhance equality and diversity achieved limited success?

Negative comments

The student could have expressed herself more logically: it is not clear whether the dramatic changes in the composition of the labour force are due to globalization or not. Compare what she wrote with the following:
The international labour force has experienced a dramatic change in its composition, particularly in terms of demographic, age, and gender (Cassell, 2006). This transition has led to diversity among employees in the workforce. The driving force behind this process is globalization, which has also brought a wide range of opportunities to economically active individuals regardless of their nationality, race or culture.
For more information on clarity, see Chapter 4.

The student chose the passive voice in this section. This is fine, but there was no need to avoid personal pronouns. In fact, the section would be more interesting if there was some variety and she had written:
'Firstly, I will give brief definitions and explanations. Secondly, I will explain two major reasons ...'
For more information on the use of personal pronouns, see Chapter 8.

Essay text

The international labour force has experienced a dramatic change in its composition, particularly in terms of demographic, age and gender (Cassell, 2006). This transition has led to diversity among employees in the workforce. Globalization has also brought a wide range of opportunities to economically active people regardless of their nationality, race or culture. However, more diversity has also meant more instances of discrimination. Diversity and equality, therefore, have become a matter of debate, attracting the attention of not only governments and corporations, but of the whole of society. It is commonly thought that real diversity and equality are difficult to achieve, and that despite a number of initiatives, success in this area has been limited.

The aim of this essay is to investigate diversity and equality in the workforce by drawing on theoretical concepts, empirical findings, policies and key actor interventions. The essay is divided into five main sections. Firstly, brief definitions and explanations of important terms are given. Secondly, two major reasons why equality and diversity need to be taken seriously are explained. Next, the causes of the difficulties in attaining equality and diversity will be examined, after which possible solutions are explored. Finally, the essay tries to give possible

Positive comments

This first sentence strikes a nice balance between general and specific. For more information on the beginning on essay, see Chapter 3.

The introduction consists of three parts, as recommended in Chapter 2. This is the first one: an explanation of the situation.

Notice how the student does not just say that there has been debate about these issues but uses 'therefore' to refer back to the evidence that has been given for this.

This is part 2 of the introduction in which the writer explains why the situation is problematic and important.

The title of the essay asks 'why', so we would expect the writer to follow a cause/effect pattern in this essay. As we said in Chapter 2, longer essays are likely to use more than one pattern, and here the writer has also included problem/solution. Notice how the student has chosen a logical structure for her essay: she makes sure that the concepts are clearly defined, then discusses the importance of the topic, the causes of the problems, some possible solutions, and then she evaluates some of these solutions.

Negative comments

Positive comments

reasons for the disappointing outcomes of equality initiatives.

> This is the third part of the introduction, in which the student states the aims and the organization of the essay.

To begin with, definitions of crucial terms are given. Equality refers to the idea of 'equal opportunity' which is defined as 'the concept of ensuring fair treatment for all employees (or prospective employees) throughout the organization' (Heery and Noon, 2001). In other words, everyone needs to be treated fairly in the workforce no matter what his/her characteristics are.

> The student has decided not to put definitions in the introduction, but in part 1 of the main body. This is a good idea here, because there are many key concepts that need to be defined. For more information on the definition of key terms and concepts, see Chapter 3.

Kandola and Fullerton (1994: 8), cited in Cassell, 2006: 346, defined managing diversity as follows:

> Notice how the quote does not interrupt the sentence and is naturally integrated.

> The block quote would look better with a line spacing of 1, rather than the 1.5 which is used throughout the essay. For more information on integrating quotes and paraphrases, see Chapter 10.

The basic concept of managing diversity accepts that the workforce consists of a diverse population of people. The diversity consists of visible and non-visible differences which will include factors such as sex, age, background, race, disability, personality and work style.

> The student was asked to use her university's version of APA referencing. For more information on referencing systems, see Chapter 9.

Put differently, diversity relates to differences among employees within an organization, whether they are noticeable or not. Usually these are the types of differences that are not of the employees' own choosing. Thompson (1997), cited in Shen et al. (2009), stated that managing diversity should be recognized as a positive organizational trait that needs to be attained, rather than a problematic issue. If diversity is well managed, everyone will feel valued, and in that way, productivity and morale alike will be enhanced; otherwise, it could lead to discrimination.

> Notice that this is a long quotation, so a block quote needed to be inserted. For more information on integrating quotes and paraphrases, see Chapter 10.

> Cautious language would be better here: 'everyone will ...' sounds too strong. An improvement would be 'employees are likely to ...' For more information on cautious language, see Chapters 3, 4 and 8.

> Notice how the student does not just quote, she comments on the quote and demonstrates that she has understood it. For more information on integrating the ideas of others, see Chapter 10.

Disadvantage refers to the lack of equal opportunities among a group of people compared with others. According to Kirton and Greene (2005: 5), there are five main social groups that are likely to be disadvantaged, namely 'women, minority ethnic people, older people, disabled people and lesbians and gay men'. Black people, for instance, have more limited access to good jobs and their average income is lower than that of white people.

> Notice that when quoting, a page number is necessary. For more information on citing and referencing, see Chapter 9.

Appendix 1 – Taking your writing up to the next level: Example essays

Negative comments

Positive comments

Notice how this paragraph starts in a more general way and then becomes specific. For more information on essay structure, see Chapter 2.

The writer should have indicated where this information comes from. For more information on deciding when to cite, see Chapter 9.

Discrimination is described as 'the process of judging people according to particular criteria' (Noon, 2010: 197). It refers to prejudice based on unfair assumptions about sex, race, age, religion and sexual orientation, and other factors, such as size or appearance. For example, in 2011, Starbucks dismissed Elsa Sallard, who has dwarfism, arguing that she posed a danger to customers and co-workers, even though she could have done her job with a stepladder. They were sued and lost their case.

In the following section, the essay investigates two major reasons why employers need to address unjust treatment, namely 'the social justice case' and 'the business case' (Noon, 2010: 200).

Notice how the student makes a smooth transition from part 1 of the main body, which includes definitions, to part 2: she announces, in more specific terms than above, what that section will contain.

The social justice case rests on the fact that the decision-making processes need to exclude 'prejudice and stereotyping', ensuring that hardly anyone feels disadvantaged or discriminated against (Noon, 2010: 201). Unfortunately, many companies use employment quota, choosing a certain percentage of various groups, such as women and black people, just to protect their good image and not because of fairness. However, basing decisions on social justice can also have a positive effect on business efficiency. The business case, therefore, needs to be taken into account.

Note the academic style, e.g. the sentence is efficient – it has no unnecessary information and uses noun structures. For more information on efficiency, see Chapter 4.

The business case is that equality and diversity could create a win–win situation for both employees and employers and their businesses (Dickens, 2005). This is due to four main reasons (Noon, 2010): managers have more recruitment choices; they can attract more talented people; sales may increase because more diversity in the workplace can lead to more diversity in the customer base; the company is presenting a positive image to its stakeholders. Moreover, costly and damaging discrimination litigation is avoided (Noon, 2010).

Despite these advantages, equality and diversity are difficult to achieve. The following section examines why.

Negative comments

Positive comments

Firstly, organizational structures and workplace culture tend to be long established and deeply embedded. Highly-paid jobs are still likely to be dominated by men (Kirton and Greene, 2000). To illustrate, the CEOs of a large number of big international corporations such as Microsoft, Google and Apple are male, and more women than men have part-time and low-paid jobs. This is related to the traditional pattern in which women raise families and do housework (Smithson and Stokoe, 2005). Other deeply-rooted attitudes are about age: older people are often considered to be less efficient and young workers are generally seen as lacking the necessary experience and qualifications. It is particularly difficult for people to find jobs or get promotions between the ages of 16 and 21 (Kirton and Greene, *ibid.*)

> Notice the good use of cautious language in this sentence.

Secondly, managers are not particularly interested in equality and diversity. Although these qualities could be beneficial for productivity and morale, they require long-term commitment, cannot be quantified financially (Dickens and Linda, 1999) and can initially be expensive, e.g. to reach a wide range of potential employees, different media need to be used. If a company is small, it could prefer to use 'word of mouth', which may constitute indirect discrimination but is much faster and cheaper (Dickens, 2005). As the priority of any organization is profit (Noon, 2010), implementing long-term strategies is often put on the back burner when managers have to deal with more urgent issues, such as competition.

> There is a citation mistake here, which the reader can easily spot: Linda is a first name. The author's name is Linda Dickens, so this should just say: (Dickens, 1999).
> For more information on authors' names, see Chapter 6.
> For more information on citing, see Chapter 9.

> This idiom could be considered too informal for an essay. The student could have written:
> As the priority of any organization is profit (Noon, 2010), more importance is usually given to urgent issues such as competition, rather than to implementing long-term strategies.
> For more information on formality, see Chapter 9.

> The student has presented the essay well: the lines all start at the same point, and the paragraphs are visually distinguished with a space. For more information on presentation, see Chapter 11.

Thirdly, equality and diversity are inherently problematic to some extent. Foster and Harris (2005) argue that not only is a diverse team difficult to manage but this also takes a toll on team coordination. Every member differs in terms of gender, age, ethnicity, schooling or skills; hence, it is hard to reach a common consensus and conflict may result. In addition, positive discrimination, which is often seen as a way to manage diversity, can lead to resentment from co-workers. For instance, parents have a right to take time off for childcare whilst those without children do not have that right, even if they have to care for elderly relatives.

> Notice how the writer makes a point and provides evidence and an explanation. For more information on the point-evidence-explanation pattern, see Chapter 6.

Appendix 1 – Taking your writing up to the next level: Example essays

Negative comments

Positive comments

There should really be a paragraph break here, to make it also visually clear that a new section is starting.
For more information about the visual aspects of paragraphing, see Chapters 2 and 11.

Notice how this paragraph is linked nicely to the previous paragraph. For more information on connecting paragraphs, see Chapter 2.

Because of these three reasons, discrimination continues to be evident in the workforce. In the following section, two key initiatives are considered: policies and positive action (Noon, 2010). Policies are undoubtedly essential in guiding managers in decision-making and taking action. Recently, many policies have been introduced in the UK, for instance the Disability Discrimination Act (1995), The Employment Equality (Religion and Belief) Regulations (2003), and The Equality Act (2006). Also, many organizations have their own formal policies. In order to ensure policy implementation, however, positive action is necessary, for example a recruitment advertisement in magazines aimed at gay people or a training programme for older employees.

Despite the presence of policies and positive action, there has been limited success in achieving equality and diversity. In the last section, this essay considers why this is so.

The first reason is the lack of intervention from pivotal actors. Dickens (1999) argues that although managers play the most crucial part, the roles of government and trade unions should not be neglected. Firstly, state intervention by legal regulation (law and policies) can contribute greatly to setting equality standards to underpin practices, regulate employer decision-making and protect employees who are discriminated against by forcing their companies to compensate them. Another actor is the trade unions, who represent employees and are responsible for protecting employee rights through collective bargaining. By negotiating with managers about certain interests or concerns of employees, collective bargaining could provide a better match between the needs of the company and employees, particularly disadvantaged groups such as ethnic minorities and women.

Whereas Dean and Liff (2010) focus on the importance of these industrial relations actors, Foster and Harris (2005) emphasize the organizational context in which both managers and external environments influence diversity practices. They give an example of a store in Leicester which tried to recruit Asian people but no one applied because they said that it was dominated by white people.

Negative comments   **Positive comments**

Another issue is that the policies of many
organizations are 'empty shells' (Hoque and Noon,
2004). There is a large gap between policies, which

The author's name is
misspelled.

are just declarations, and action (Dickens, 2005).
According to Dicken (2005), 27% of company
with policies had not implemented them. In
addition, many managers treat everyone the same

This should say 'companies'.
For more information on the
importance of accuracy, see
Chapter 5.

without realizing that they differ in many ways,
and those differences need to be valued to improve
individual potential (Foster and Harris, 2005).

To sum up, striving for equality and diversity
should be an important consideration for
organizations. If this is done well, it will be
beneficial to both organizations and employees
in terms of productivity and efficiency. However,
this is difficult to achieve for a number of
reasons, including deep-rooted prejudice,
managerial priorities and the side-effects of
positive discrimination. There are two possible
paths towards equality and diversity: policies and
positive action. However, without the efforts of
key protagonists such as the government, trade
unions and employees, any initiatives are likely to
have limited success. Other obstacles are a lack of
managerial goodwill and company culture. In order
to eradicate disadvantage, a number of factors need
to be combined: the social justice approach, the
business approach, national legislation and local
policies and action.

Notice how the student
demonstrates her awareness
of what her tutor wants: she
has clearly given an answer
to the essay question here.
For more information about
analysing essay titles, see
Chapter 1.

The last sentence focuses on
possible solutions, and can
be regarded as the overall
conclusion. The other two
parts of conclusions are
also in this paragraph:
summaries of the main ideas
and evidence.
For more information on
essay structure, see
Chapter 2.
For information about
the language used in
conclusions, see Chapter 3.

Appendix 1 – Taking your writing up to the next level: Example essays

Negative comments

REFERENCE LIST

Positive comments

Cassell, C., 'Managing Diversity', in T. Redman and A. Wilkinson, *Contemporary Human Resource Management* (3rd edn., London: Prentice Hall, 2006), 343–360.

Dean, D. and Liff, S., 'Equality and diversity: The ultimate industrial relations concern', in T. Colling and M. Terry, *Industrial Relations* (Oxford: Wiley-Blackwell, 2010), 422–446.

> *Dickens and Linda. This should say: Dickens, L.*

Dickens and Linda, 'Beyond the business case: A three-pronged approach to equality action', in *Human Resource Management Journal* (1999), **9** (1), 9–19.

Dickens, L., 'Walking the talk? Equality and diversity in employment', in S. Bach, *Managing Human Resources* (Oxford: Blackwell, 2005), 178–203.

> *Human resource management Journal … The whole title needs to be capitalized: Human Resource Management Journal*

Foster, C. and Harris, L., 'Easy to say, difficult to do: diversity management in retail', in *Human resource management Journal* (2005), **15** (3), 4–17.

Heery, E. and Noon, M., *A Dictionary of Human Resource Management* (Oxford: Oxford University Press, 2001).

Hoque, K. and Noon, M., 'Equal Opportunities Policy and Practice in Britain: Evaluating the 'empty shell' hypothesis', in *Work, Employment and Society* (2004), **18** (3), 481–506.

> *Janet Smithson and Elizabeth H. Stokoe. The first names of the authors should not be included: Smithson, J. and Stokoe, E.*

Janet Smithson and Elizabeth H. Stokoe, 'Gender, Work and Organization', in *Discourses of Work-Life Balance: Negotiating 'Genderblind' Terms in Organizations* (2005), **12** (2), 147–168.

Kirton, G. and Greene, A., *The Dynamics of Managing Diversity: A Critical Approach* (Oxford: Butterworth-Heinemann, 2000).

Noon, M., 'Managing equality and diversity', in J. Beardwell and T. Claydon, *Human Resource Management: A Contemporary Approach* (London: Pearson, 2010), 196–229.

Shen, J., Chanda, A., D'Netto, B. and Monga, M., 'Managing diversity through human resource management: an international perspective and conceptual framework', in *The International Journal of Human Resource Management*, (2009), **20** (2), 235–251.

> *The reference list is started on a new page, as it should be. All the names mentioned in the text are represented in the reference list and vice versa. The student seems to have followed her university's style guide and has used identical patterns for the same types of sources. All the sources she has used are academic sources. For more information on academic sources, see Chapter 6. For more information on reference lists, see Chapter 9.*

Appendix 2 – Responding to marking criteria and feedback

When you receive your essay title, you are often given information about how you should deal with it, for example 'Use a variety of sources', 'Refer to your lecture notes', 'Include at least three theories'. You need to follow these instructions carefully, as your mark will depend on your ability to do so.

It is also important to read or print off any other information provided by your department. This could cover presentation requirements, referencing systems, etc. and may be found online (via the university website or their virtual learning environment) or in a handbook or other document.

You may also be given marking criteria, which state what the marker will be looking for in your work. This may include wording such as 'evidence of reading', 'the ability to incorporate the ideas of others', 'a demonstration of knowledge', 'an ability to apply knowledge', 'the ability to consider and discuss different points of view', etc. Again, keep this in mind while you are putting your essay together. When you have finished your first draft you need to double check that there is evidence of these skills in the essay.

Unfortunately, many students find it difficult to understand what is meant by some of these criteria. You will become better at this through practice, but you can speed up this process by examining the feedback you get on your essays, both the positive and the negative comments. As we saw in Chapter 11, analysing essay feedback can be considered a stage of the essay writing process. It needs to be seen as guidance for your next essay.

Have a look at the following paragraph, taken from an essay on relationship and transactional marketing. Look at the lecturer's notes in the margin. Before you read on, consider what the student can do to understand what is wrong in this essay and what he should do before writing his next one.

Relationship marketing can be defined as 'attracting new customers, obtaining and maintaining the relationships between original customers and companies' (J.A.F. Nicholls, 2000). This strategy focuses on keeping in touch with customers, especially the loyal customers, rather than concentrating on individual sales. Gronroon's (1996) definition of relationship marketing strategy is 'to build, maintain and proceed the relationships between customers and relative shareholders, while to terminate collaboration when it is necessary'. It can be seen that relationship marketing is based on the exchange and promise between customers and firms. This strategy incorporates the 4Cs marketing mix and has long-term benefits.	*(1) reference format* *(2) is this the author's name?* *(3) page number? exact quote?* *(4) is this the only definition?* *(5) good insight, but could be developed further* *(6) explain*

The student did not follow referencing conventions: he misspelled an author's name, gave initials in citation, may have misquoted an author and did not include a page reference for his quote. Although comments (1) and (3) do not say exactly what is wrong, the student should have more information that he can consult, possibly online, in the form of his department's guidelines for academic writing. If this does not exist then he would have to make an appointment to see his tutor.

Comment (4) suggests that there are more definitions, which means that the student should have read more and not stopped his research as soon as he found one definition. A library search on the topic of 'relationship marketing' would have shown more than one source.

Comment (5) includes positive feedback. Next time, the student should therefore try to give more comments about the quotes that he uses. The lecturer seems to appreciate it when the student shows his personal understanding of the definition, and wants him to keep adding insights like this and developing them further.

Comment (6) suggests that there is more to say about the 4Cs, and that 'long-term benefits' needs an explanation too.

Now look at some comments taken from the feedback that the lecturer provided at the end of the essay. Notice how many of the comments can actually be linked to what the lecturer had put in the margin above. They have been numbered below to make it easier for you to find them.

> - You demonstrated that you understood (5) the concepts related to relationship marketing and transactional marketing, but this could have been explored in more depth (5), by analysing and synthesizing a number of different authors' opinions (4) and drawing your own conclusions (5). Make sure you always back up your statements and opinions with clarifications or evidence (6), as these will strengthen your arguments.
>
> - Unfortunately, you did not follow referencing conventions (1, 2, 3), which is not acceptable at this stage.
>
> - Perhaps in part 2 you could have given more examples of how transactional marketing has been beneficial to the companies you mention.

In short, don't glance over the comments that have been put on your essay and then put them away. Instead, spend time on really trying to understand them. It can be painful to read the comments if your results are not what you had hoped for, but it is time well spent if it can help you learn from your mistakes.

Have a look at a paragraph written by a Social Policy student. Read the comments that the tutor made and decide whether these are positive, neutral or negative comments. Before you read on, think about how important it is to avoid similar issues in the next essay.

One of Ponzini and Rossi's (2010) approaches is to critically discuss Florida's theory and the problems caused by the application of his theory to urban policy. They explain how an unclear theory or its incorrect interpretation by misunderstood politicians could cause social-spatial injustice. This is because city development is related to the exchange of policy models aiming to ensure the comprehensiveness and role of each city in the world (Sassen, 1994). Ponzini and Rossi look at specific cities and specifically their urban and spatial restructure and policies. However, it could be argued that looking at individual cases may not be appropriate, due to the cities' diversity. This would mean applying a multi-case study for finding a paradigm via exemplary samples (Gibson and Kong, 2005).	*(1) do they have another approach?* *(2) are the politicians misunderstood?* *(3) it might have been a good idea to have explained the link between politicians and policy models* *(4) comprehensiveness?* *(5) you could have given some examples of cities here* *(6) This = ?* *(7) perhaps you could have referred here to some later studies by the same authors*

In general, when a lecturer uses language such as '**perhaps** you **could have**', 'it **might** have been a good idea to', or asks questions, they are using polite language to tell you what you **should** have done. Don't ignore comments like these: they are not about possibilities or queries, but tell you what you should have done to get a better mark. Do not treat any comments as 'neutral' comments or small points. Instead, think about the underlying issues and take them into consideration for your next essay. Let's have a look at the specific examples.

Comment (1) suggests that there is no other approach, and that the student should have written 'Ponzini and Rossi's (2010) approach is …', in which case the underlying problem is a lack of clarity in the language. The other possibility is that the problem is with setting up the wrong reader expectation: the reader expects to hear what the other approaches are, but the student never picks up that point in the assignment.

Comment (2) is not a real question: the tutor knows that the politicians are not misunderstood: the politicians misunderstand the policy and it is the policy that is misunderstood. The question points out to the student that there is a language problem.

In (3), (5) and (7) polite language is being used to say that the student **should** have done something (explain, give examples, include more studies). In other words, the student has not researched deeply or widely enough, understood enough of the research or selected the right information.

Comments (4) and (6) can be read as requests for clarification. It can be frustrating for students to see question marks in their work without further explanation, but usually it just means that the meaning of a phrase or sentence has not been made clear enough. It is important for the writer to put themselves in the shoes of the reader, to see if what has been written makes sense. Here 'comprehensiveness' is a concept that needs further explanation in the context of cities, and 'this' does not seem to relate to anything in the previous sentence.

To sum up, you probably receive more information than you realize about how you can achieve higher grades. The trick is to pay careful attention. If, despite your efforts, you still really don't understand specific criteria or feedback, don't be afraid to say so and ask your lecturer to explain verbally.

Some final words from the author

This book has given you a lot of advice about the different requirements of essay writing, and you may feel that there is so much that it is not possible for you to follow it all. Luckily, that is not necessary. Instead of worrying about all the guidelines, focus on the bigger picture using the following checklist:

- Does the essay answer the question?

- Will my reader understand what I am trying to do and say?

- Is it clear what my opinion is?

- Is it clear where I have given the opinion of others?

- Have I expressed myself clearly, formally, efficiently, modestly and accurately?

- Have I followed the other academic conventions?

It is also worth remembering that lecturers tend to start you off with the easier essays, that there is support available from individuals and departments at your institution, and that nobody expects you to get everything right from the start. Take the results from your first essay as a starting point and, most importantly, study the feedback to help you improve. Be proud of your hard work, and of every pass, merit and distinction you receive.

Els Van Geyte

Appendix 3 – Useful phrases

Useful phrases introduced throughout the book are reproduced here for easy reference.

Linkers
Sequencing

- Firstly, ... /
  First of all, ...

- Secondly, ...

- Finally, ...

Adding ideas

- In addition, ...

- Also, ...

- Furthermore, ...

- Moreover, ...

Contrasting ideas

- On the one hand, ...
  On the other hand, ...

- However, ...

- Although ...

- In contrast, ...

- Whilst

Talking about results

- Therefore, ...

- As a consequence, ... / Consequently, ...

Talking about causes

- Due to ...

- As a consequence of ...

Referring back to a previous point

- This analysis (suggests that ...)

- This approach (indicates that ...)

- This concept (illustrates that ...)

- This context (shows that ...)

- These data (prove that ...)

- This definition (has been used to ...)

- These factors (need to be taken into account when ...)

- This interpretation (is influenced by ...)

- This period (was characterized by ...)

- This process (can be seen in ...)

- This response (was summarized by ...)

- This sector (was restructured in …)
- This theory (was widely debated by …)
- These guiding principles (throw light on …)
- Another argument (in favour of the privatization …)

Giving definitions

- (Synthesis) is (the process of combining objects or ideas into a complex whole).
- (Synthesis) is commonly defined as (the process of combining objects or ideas into a complex whole).
- (Synthesis) is generally understood to refer to (the process of combining objects or ideas into a complex whole).
- (Synthesis) can be described as (the process of combining objects or ideas into a complex whole).
- (The process of combining objects or ideas into a complex whole) is called (synthesis).
- (The process of combining objects or ideas into a complex whole) is known as (synthesis).
- (The process of combining objects or ideas into a complex whole) is referred to as (synthesis).

Using definitions

- For the purposes of this essay, I will be using (Kotler's definition of societal marketing), because of (its focus on the organization's task to meet the need …)
- Although many different definitions (of marketing) have been suggested (over the years), I will be using (the one by Kotler (1994), because of …)
- Throughout this essay, I will be using the word ('cognitive') to refer to (the different types of intellectual behaviour).
- (In this essay), the term ('reliability') is used to mean …

Indicating the importance of the topic

- (One of) the most significant (stages in a child's development) is …
- (One of) the most important (factors to take into consideration when …) is …
- (One of) the most essential (conditions for the germination of orchidea) is …
- (Some of) the most memorable aspects (of the documentary) were …

Intensifying adjectives

- an important part
- a key role/factor
- a great/major problem
- a central area of
- a common problem
- an increasing need/concern
- heightened awareness
- rapid development

- a dramatic increase
- renewed/unprecedented interest

- a serious effect/impact on
- increasing concern

Introducing the aim and the organization of the essay

- This essay will …
- This report attempts to (examine whether …)
- This case study hopes to (determine whether …)
- The aims of this essay are to (determine whether …)
- This essay examines whether (the effects of exposure to …)
- This essay argues that (the effects of exposure to …)
- In this essay I argue that (the historical influences of …)
- In this essay I will discuss (the origins of …)
- In this essay it will be argued that (the Middle Ages were …)

The language of conclusions

- This essay discussed (the economic factors that contributed to …)
- In this essay, I have argued (that globalization is not a recent phenomenon).
- This essay has explored (the causes of the conflict …)
- These findings suggest that (bees are nearing extinction).
- The evidence seems to indicate that (prolonged bouts of laughter lead to …)
- A consequence of this is that (Western lifestyles have become more fashionable).

Counter-argumentation

- One study has emphasized the need for (a change in the way custody cases are …)
- So far there has been limited agreement only on (three of the proposed laws).
- Some studies have challenged (this concept).
- There is continuing debate about the value of (trialling this vaccine in …)
- The literature shows some contradictory findings (in this area).

Claims the author makes

- There are several drawbacks (involved in investing in …)
- There is not enough reliable evidence that (ingesting valium results in …)

- These are the most dangerous substances (on the face of the earth, yet ...)

- One of the most significant patterns is (also one of the easiest to disrupt).

The use of 'I' and 'we' to indicate the writer's stance

- My concern is ...

- My definition ... is based on Munson's but combines this with ...

- Experiments have been carried out by Nelson and Smith (1993) and Ojha and Mazumder (2008). In our experiment ...

- We know that ... has consequences ... that are still apparent ... today ...

- As we have seen, ...

Quoting
Wood (2011: 23) describes their textile industry as "flourishing", yet some analysts are indicating that it is in decline.

Paraphrasing
Whereas Wood (2011) has a positive view of the current state of their textile industry, some analysts are indicating that it is in decline.

Reporting verbs

- They discussed / examined (the potential problems with this type of test).

- The authors show / report (how technology is being used to engage students more).

- They suggest that / how (these data could be interpreted in different ways).

- They suggest (a different interpretation of the data).

- It was alleged that (the copyright for the image wasn't cleared).

- They claimed to have (informed their neighbours of their intention).

- The head of education proposed (a set of new measures to guard against bullying).

- The report acknowledges that (the proposed building plot was not suitable).

- The research demonstrates that (it is dependent on a low percentage of imports).

- The curator of the exhibition asserts that (Manet was the founder of modernism).

Glossary

Some of the more difficult words from the chapters are defined here in this Glossary. The definitions focus on the meanings of the words in the context in which they appear in the text. Definitions are from *COBUILD Advanced Dictionary*.

Key

ADJ	adjective	N-UNCOUNT	uncount noun
ADV	adverb	N-VAR	variable noun
AUX	auxiliary verb	NEG	negative
COLOUR	colour word	NUM	number
COMB	combining form	ORD	ordinal
CONJ	conjunction	PASSIVE	see V-PASSIVE
CONVENTION	convention	PHRASAL VERB	phrasal verb
DET	determiner	PHRASE	phrase
EXCLAM	exclamation	PREDET	predeterminer
FRACTION	fraction	PREFIX	prefix
LINK	see V-LINK	PREP	preposition
MODAL	modal verb	PRON	pronoun
N-COUNT	count noun	QUANT	quantifier
N-PLURAL	plural noun	QUEST	question word
N-PROPER	proper noun	SUFFIX	suffix
N-PROPER-PLURAL	plural proper noun	VERB	verb
N-SING	singular noun	V-LINK	link verb
N-TITLE	title noun	V-PASSIVE	passive verb

a

abbreviation (abbreviations) N-COUNT
An abbreviation is a short form of a word or phrase, made by leaving out some of the letters or by using only the first letter of each word.

accountable ADJ
If you are accountable to someone for something that you do, you are responsible for it and must be prepared to justify your actions to that person.

accuracy N-UNCOUNT
The accuracy of information or measurements is their quality of being true or correct, even in small details.

acronym (acronyms) N-COUNT
An acronym is a word composed of the first letters of the words in a phrase, especially when this is used as a name. An example of an acronym is NATO which is made up of the first letters of the 'North Atlantic Treaty Organization'.

active (actives) N-COUNT
An active, active verb, or active form, is the form of the verb which is used when the subject refers to a person or thing that does something. For example, in 'I saw her yesterday', the verb is in the active.

adverbial ADJ
Adverbial means relating to adverbs or like an adverb.

allocate (allocates, allocating, allocated) VERB
If one item or share of something is allocated to a particular person or for a particular purpose, it is given to that person or used for that purpose.

analogy (analogies) N-COUNT
If you make or draw an analogy between two things, you show that they are similar in some way.

anatomically ADV
If the body of a person or an animal is anatomically large, it is physically or structurally large.

anonymous ADJ
Something that is anonymous does not reveal who you are.

anti-discrimination ADJ
An anti-discrimination action is an action that shows that you are opposed to the practice of treating one person or group of people less fairly or less well than other people or groups.

appendix (appendices) N-COUNT
An appendix to a book or essay is extra information that is placed after the end of the main text.

argument (arguments) N-VAR
An argument is a statement or set of statements that you use in order to try to convince people that your opinion about something is correct.

assert (asserts, asserting, asserted) VERB
If someone asserts a fact or belief, they state it firmly.

assignment (assignments) N-COUNT
An assignment is a task or piece of work that you are given to do, especially as part of your job or studies.

attribute to (attributes to, attributing to, attributed to) VERB
If you attribute something to an event or situation, you think that it was caused by that event or situation.

authoritative ADJ
Someone or something that is authoritative has a lot of knowledge of a particular subject.

authority N-UNCOUNT
If someone speaks or writes with authority, people respect and take notice of what they say because they have special knowledge of a subject.

b

balanced ADJ
A balanced report, book, or other document takes into account all the different opinions on something and presents information in a fair and reasonable way.

blues N-PLURAL
If you have got the blues, you feel depressed.

bright (brighter, brightest) ADJ
If you describe a person or an animal as bright, you mean that they are quick at learning things.

c

caption (captions) N-COUNT
A caption is the words printed underneath or above a picture or table which explain what it is about.

catwalk (catwalks) N-COUNT
At a fashion show, the catwalk is a narrow platform that models walk along to display clothes.

cautious ADJ
If you describe someone's attitude, language, or reaction as cautious, you mean that it is limited or careful.

charity (charities) N-COUNT
A charity is an organization which raises money in order to help people who are ill, disabled, or very poor.

chronological ADJ
If things are described or shown in chronological order, they are described or shown in the order in which they happened.

cite (cites, citing, cited) VERB
If you cite something, you quote it or mention it, especially as an example or proof of what you are saying.

clarity N-UNCOUNT
The clarity of something such as a book or argument is its quality of being well explained and easy to understand.

classify (classifies, classifying, classified) VERB
To classify things means to divide them into groups or types so that things with similar characteristics are in the same group.

cohesion N-UNCOUNT
If you write with cohesion, you use language that shows that the different aspects of your writing relate to each other, fit together well, and form a united whole.

collaborative writing N-UNCOUNT
Collaborative writing is writing done by two or more people or groups working together.

compile (compiles, compiling, compiled) VERB
When you compile something such as a report, book, or table, you produce it by collecting and putting together many pieces of information.

complement (complements) N-COUNT
The complement of a link verb is an adjective group or noun group which comes after the verb and describes or identifies the subject. For example, in the sentence 'They felt very tired', 'very tired' is the complement. In 'They were students', 'students' is the complement.

constitute (constitutes, constituting, constituted) V-LINK
If something constitutes a particular thing, it can be regarded as being that thing.

context (contexts) N-VAR
The context of a word, sentence, or text consists of the words, sentences, or text before and after it which help to make its meaning clear.

convention (conventions) N-COUNT
Academic conventions are traditional methods or styles of academic writing.

convey (conveys, conveying, conveyed) VERB
To convey information or feelings means to cause them to be known or understood by someone.

corporate governance N-UNCOUNT
Corporate governance is the way in which a business corporation is managed.

creditor (creditors) N-COUNT
Your creditors are the people who you owe money to.

criteria (criterion) N-PLURAL
Criteria are factors on which you decide or judge something.

critique (critiques) N-COUNT
A critique is a written examination and judgment of a situation or of a person's work or ideas.

d

defining relative clause (defining relative clauses) N-COUNT
A defining relative clause is a subordinate clause which gives information about a person or thing, explaining or specifying which person or thing you are talking about.

deliberate ADJ
If you do something that is deliberate, you planned or decided to do it beforehand, and so it happens on purpose rather than by chance.

demonstrative adjective (demonstrative adjectives) N-COUNT
Demonstrative adjectives are the words 'this', 'that', 'these', and 'those'.

dense (denser, densest) ADJ
If a text or sentence is dense, it contains a lot of information in a small or short space.

design specification (design specifications) N-COUNT
A design specification is a clearly stated requirement about the necessary features in the design of something.

determiner (determiners) N-COUNT
A determiner is a word which is used at the beginning of a noun group to indicate, for example, which thing you are referring to or whether you are referring to one thing or several. Common English determiners are 'a', 'the', 'some', 'this', and 'each'.

discipline (disciplines) N-COUNT
A discipline is a particular area of study, especially a subject of study in a college or university.

dissertation (dissertations) N-COUNT
A dissertation is a long formal piece of writing on a particular subject, especially for a university degree.

distinguish (distinguishes, distinguishing, distinguished) VERB
If you distinguish one thing from another or distinguish between two things, you show, see, or understand how they are different.

drawback (drawbacks) N-COUNT
A drawback is an aspect of something or someone that makes them less acceptable than they would otherwise be.

dualist ADJ
If a person or their way of thinking is dualist, they believe that something has two main parts or aspects.

e

efficiency N-UNCOUNT
Efficiency is the quality of being able to do a task successfully, without repetition or wasting time or energy.

ethical ADJ
Ethical means relating to beliefs about right and wrong.

exemplify (exemplifies, exemplifying, exemplified) VERB
If you exemplify something you are saying or writing, you give an example to make it clearer.

expulsion (expulsions) N-VAR
Expulsion is when someone is forced to leave a school, university, or organization.

f

fatigue N-UNCOUNT
Fatigue in metal or wood is a weakness in it that is caused by repeated stress. Fatigue can cause the metal or wood to break.

feminist empiricism N-UNCOUNT
Feminist empiricism is the belief that people should rely on practical experience and experiments, rather than theories, as a basis for knowledge, and that these should not favour or be concerned with one gender more than the other.

figure (figures) N-COUNT
In books, journal articles, and essays, the diagrams which help to show or explain information are referred to as figures.

flow chart (flow charts) N-COUNT
A flow chart or a flow diagram is a diagram which represents the sequence of actions in a particular process or activity.

footnote (footnotes) N-COUNT
A footnote is a note at the bottom of a page in a book which provides more detailed information about something that is mentioned on that page.

formality N-UNCOUNT
If you talk about the formality of a person's language or writing style, you mean that they are using extremely formal academic language.

further (furthers, furthering, furthered) VERB
If you further something, you help it to progress, to be successful, or to be achieved.

g

genre (genres) N-COUNT
A genre is a particular type of literature, painting, music, film, or other art form which people consider as a class because it has special characteristics.

geological ADJ
Geological means relating to geology.

get into (gets into, getting into, got into) PHRASAL VERB
If you get into a particular kind of work or activity, you manage to become involved in it.

guild (guilds) N-COUNT
A guild is an organization of people who do the same job or activity.

i

immune response (immune responses) N-COUNT
Your immune response is the reaction of your body to the presence of substances causing disease or infection.

immunity N-UNCOUNT
If you talk about someone's immunity to a particular disease, you mean that they cannot be affected by it.

indent (indents) N-COUNT
An indent is the space at the beginning of a line of writing when it starts further away from the edge of the paper than all the other lines.

initiative (initiatives) N-COUNT
An initiative is an important act or statement that is intended to solve a problem.

innovation N-UNCOUNT
Innovation is the introduction of new ideas, methods, or things.

inspiration N-UNCOUNT
Inspiration is a feeling of enthusiasm you get from someone or something, which gives you new and creative ideas.

integrate (integrates, integrating, integrated) VERB
If you integrate one thing with another, or one thing integrates with another, the two things become closely linked or form part of a whole idea or system. You can also say that two things integrate.

integrity N-UNCOUNT
If you have integrity in academic writing, you are honest about what is your point of view and what is the point of view of other people.

intent (intents) N-VAR
If you state your intent in a piece of writing, you say what you intend to do in the writing.

invalidation N-UNCOUNT
The invalidation of someone's academic qualifications is a declaration that they are no longer valid.

irrelevant ADJ
If you describe something such as a fact or remark as irrelevant, you mean that it is not connected with what you are discussing or dealing with.

j

justification N-UNCOUNT
If you use left or right justification when you lay out printed text, you begin each line at the same distance from the left-hand or right-hand edge of the page or column.

k

key word (key words) N-COUNT
Key words in a text are the most important words used in discussing a topic.

l

lab report (lab reports) N-COUNT
A lab report is a document which you write after doing an experiment or investigating a situation in a laboratory.

linear ADJ
A linear process or development is one in which something changes or progresses straight from one stage to another, and has a starting point and an ending point.

literature review (literature reviews) N-COUNT
If you do a literature review, you read relevant literature such as books and journal articles so that you have a good, basic knowledge of a topic.

m

measure (measures) N-COUNT
When someone, usually a government or other authority, takes measures to do something, they carry out particular actions in order to achieve a particular result.

metaphor (metaphors) N-VAR
A metaphor is an imaginative way of describing something by referring to something else which is the same in a particular way. For example, if you want to say that someone is very shy and frightened of things, you might say that they are a mouse.

microfinance N-UNCOUNT
Microfinance is the lending of money to unemployed people or people or groups that have a low income, and who may not usually be able to borrow money.

modesty N-UNCOUNT
If you write with modesty, you use impersonal and cautious language in your writing.

module (modules) N-COUNT
A module is one of the separate parts of a course taught at a college or university.

morality N-UNCOUNT
The morality of something is how right or acceptable it is.

n

neutral ADJ-GRADED
If someone uses neutral language, they choose words which do not indicate that they approve or disapprove of something.

o

objective ADJ
If someone is objective, they base their opinions on facts rather than on their personal feelings.

obstacle (obstacles) N-COUNT
You can refer to anything that makes it difficult for you to do something as an obstacle.

outline (outlines) N-VAR
An outline is a general explanation or description of something.

p

paraphrasing N-UNCOUNT
Paraphrasing is when you express what someone else has said or written in a different way.

passive (passives) N-COUNT
A passive, passive form, or passive verb is formed using 'be' and the past participle of a verb. The subject of a passive clause does not perform the action expressed by the verb but is affected by it. For example, in 'He's been murdered', the verb is in the passive.

pedagogy N-UNCOUNT
Pedagogy is the study and theory of the methods and principles of teaching.

phrasal verb (phrasal verbs) N-COUNT
A phrasal verb is a combination of a verb and an adverb or preposition, for example 'shut up' or 'look after', which together have a particular meaning.

policy (policies) N-VAR
A policy is a set of ideas or plans that is used as a basis for making decisions, especially in politics, economics, or business.

possession N-UNCOUNT
Possession is the state of having something because you have obtained it or because it belongs to you.

possessive (possessives) N-COUNT
A possessive is a word such as 'my' or 'his' which shows who or what something belongs to or is connected with, or the possessive form of a name or noun which has 's added to it, as in 'Jenny's' or 'cat's'.

post-modern ADJ
Post-modern is used to describe something or someone that is influenced by post-modernism.

post-modernism N-UNCOUNT
Post-modernism is a late twentieth century approach in art, architecture, and literature which typically mixes styles, ideas, and references to modern society, often in an ironic way.

PR N-UNCOUNT
PR is an abbreviation for public relations. Public relations is the part of an organization's work that is concerned with obtaining the public's approval for what it does.

preliminary ADJ
Preliminary activities or discussions take place at the beginning of an event, often as a form of preparation.

principle (principles) N-COUNT
The principles of a particular theory or philosophy are its basic rules or laws.

procrastination N-UNCOUNT
Procrastination is when you keep leaving things you should do until later, often because you do not want to do them.

proofreading N-UNCOUNT
Proofreading is the act of reading through a book, an article, or an essay before it is submitted or published in order to find and mark mistakes that need to be corrected.

proposal (proposals) N-COUNT
A proposal is a plan or an idea, often a formal or written one, which is suggested for people to think about and decide upon.

provoke (provokes, provoking, provoked) VERB
If something provokes a question, reaction, or effect, it causes the question to be asked, causes a particular reaction, or has a particular effect.

r

reference work (reference works) N-COUNT
A reference work is a book, journal, or article that you look at when you need specific information or facts about a subject.

reliable ADJ
Information that is reliable or that is from a reliable source is very likely to be correct.

research report (research reports) NOUN
A research report is a document that you write which shows the results of your research.

respectively ADV
Respectively means in the same order as the items that you have just mentioned.

s

saying (sayings) N-COUNT
A saying is a sentence that people often say and that gives advice or information about human life and experience.

scandal (scandals) N-COUNT
A scandal is a situation or event that is thought to be shocking and immoral and that everyone knows about.

search term (search terms) N-COUNT
A search term is a word or phrase that you put
into a database or search engine in order to
find information, books, or journal articles that
contain or deal with a particular subject.

sector (sectors) N-COUNT
A particular sector of a country's economy is
the part connected with that specified type of
industry.

seminar (seminars) N-COUNT
A seminar is a class at a college or university in
which the teacher and a small group of students
discuss a topic.

shareholder (shareholders) N-COUNT
A shareholder is a person who owns shares in a
company.

sophistication N-UNCOUNT
Sophistication is the quality of being more
advanced or complex than other things.

specification (specifications) N-COUNT
A specification is a requirement which is clearly
stated, for example about the necessary features
in the design of something.

spidergram (spidergrams) N-COUNT
A spidergram is a drawing to show facts or ideas,
which has the main topic in a circle in the centre
with other important facts on lines drawn out
from this central circle.

stakeholder (stakeholders) N-COUNT
Stakeholders are people who have an interest in a
company's or organization's affairs.

stance (stances) N-COUNT
Your stance on a particular matter is your attitude
to it.

sub-clause (sub-clauses) N-COUNT
A sub-clause or subordinate clause is a clause
in a sentence which adds to or completes the
information given in the main clause. It cannot
usually stand alone as a sentence.

synonym (synonyms) N-COUNT
A synonym is a word or expression which means
the same as another word or expression.

synthesis (syntheses) N-COUNT
A synthesis of different ideas or styles is a mixture
or combination of these ideas or styles.

t

tentative ADJ
Tentative answers, plans, or arrangements are not
definite or certain, but have been given or made
as a first step.

tone N-SING
The tone of a speech or piece of writing is its style
and the opinions or ideas expressed in it.

trial and error PHRASE
If you do something by trial and error, you try
several different methods of doing it until you
find the method that works properly.

v

verify (verifies, verifying, verified) VERB
If you verify something, you check that it is true by
careful examination or investigation.

Answer key

Chapter 1

Exercise 1

1, 4 = give different points of view (and your opinion)

2, 3 = write about, describe

When answering questions 2 and 3 you will have to describe what (might have) happened. Questions 1 and 4 are more about opinions about how far something is true ('less', 'sufficiently') and the terminology used is open to interpretation ('effective', 'advanced').

Notice how the meaning of a word depends on the context. Different disciplines may have different ways of using words, and you need to think about what happens in yours. Looking at example essays or exam questions from previous years can help.

Exercise 2

1 c 2 a 3 f 4 h 5 b 6 d
7 e 8 j 9 g 10 i

Exercise 3

a The topic is 'urban planning theories'.

b There are three sentences, without major subdivisions.

c

Part	Instruction	What I should do
1	What are the key urban planning theories that have emerged in the post-war period?	■ say what the most important (= 'key')urban planning theories are, but ONLY mention the ones that were developed after the war
2	Outline in summary their key characteristics.	■ for each theory, give the main characteristics ONLY, WITHOUT going into detail
3	With reference to one of these theories, explain how they help us understand the nature of planning practice.	■ choose one theory ■ explain how this theory relates to practice by answering the question: 'How does the theory enable an understanding of the nature of planning practice?'

Exercise 4

1 C

2 B

Exercise 5

1, 2, 3 ✔

'appreciation of politics' ?

The question says … ✗

There is a danger here that the student is going in the wrong direction.

The question could be reformulated as follows: 'Is it absolutely necessary to understand politics in order to understand opportunities and constraints for development? Select a country and analyse their understanding (of politics and the opportunities/constraints for development). Use development theory in your analysis and other academic sources about development.'

The student does not seem to understand the meaning of 'appreciation'. The reason for this may be the fact that the word has different meanings. Have a look at the four dictionary definitions and decide which one is most likely here:

A Appreciation of something is the recognition and enjoyment of its good qualities.

B Your appreciation for something that someone does for you is your gratitude for it.

C An appreciation of a situation is an understanding of what it involves.

D Appreciation in the value of something is an increase in its value over a period of time.

The closest meaning here is C, an understanding. The best dictionary to use for most academic purposes is an Advanced Learner's Dictionary. We have used the *Collins COBUILD Advanced Dictionary* here.

The reason that the lecturer uses 'thinkers' separately from 'development theory' is probably because not all thinkers have come up with whole theories. The student needs to look at what thinkers have said about development and that includes looking at development theory. It is unlikely that 'thinker' and 'theory' are seen as two completely separate concepts.

Chapter 2

Exercise 1
Suggested answers:

Introduction	background: urban planning in the post-war period
Main body	■ describe the most important planning theories in this period (main characteristics) ■ explain one theory in more detail ■ relate this theory to practice: explain how it helps us understand the nature of planning practice
Conclusion	summarizing comments about urban planning in the post-war period and the link between theory and practice

Exercise 2
This is what we would expect a student to do in an introduction:

1 give a description or explanation of the situation or problem (more general)

2 say why this problem (or a more specific aspect of it) is important

3 say what the organization of your essay will be.

Introduction A
The writer of Introduction A has demonstrated that she understands the question: we know that she understands the meaning of 'discuss' in this context as she immediately starts talking about benefits and drawbacks. She also clearly indicates the structure of the essay (point 3): 'first ... the role calculators play ... benefits ... drawbacks ... Then ... argument for ... by examining ... before concluding ...'.

What she has not done is explore the situation (point 1) and show why this question is worth discussing (point 2). It may be that historically, calculators have been used as soon as they were affordable, or this may have started because of educational theories that suggested that they were necessary, or perhaps this is a cultural issue and in some countries they are not allowed to be used. Once this background is provided, the student could then have explained why it is an issue that is worth discussing: are there different educational theories, cultural shifts, studies that suggest calculators should not be used? Although she should not go into these issues in depth, she could have used them to justify why this topic is worth discussing.

In this particular case, she nearly did this: there is a suggestion that the question has to be discussed in the context of the purpose of an educational system – but she should have said more about this.

Introduction B
This student includes point (2): he is saying why this particular question is being raised and is therefore worthy of discussion. In the last sentence, he also says (as student 1 did) whether he agrees or disagrees with the comment.

It is a good idea to 'answer' the question. Not only does it show that you understand what the question is, but it also tells your reader what you are going to argue, which guides them through your text.

This student has not really included enough for point 1, and there is no comment about organization (point 3).

We can take the best from both introductions to write a better one:

Calculators are useful pieces of equipment and are commonly used in classrooms all over the world. Recently, however, a number of studies (*you would insert the details here – see information about references in Chapter 9*) have questioned the role of the calculator in the primary school classroom, suggesting that it may slow students' ability to understand mathematical concepts. This essay will first address the role calculators play by examining some established benefits as well as the drawbacks mentioned in the recent research. It will then discuss the underlying purpose of all educational systems before concluding that calculators will always have a use in learning environments.

Exercise 3

(1) In conclusion, new technologies have provided a remarkable breakthrough which has allowed society itself to become incredibly advanced. (2) They have now become so highly developed that they have provoked ethical questions about their morality. One of the main reasons for this is that they can be controlling, but as we have seen, they are liberating at the same time, with cyborg (mechanical body parts) technology even being able to save people's lives. Another area of thought is related to the area of feminism: despite their large contribution to the fields of science and technology, women still have to struggle with inequality in everyday and scientific life. While new technologies have undoubtedly influenced postmodern thinking, (3) the amount of research activity in the field in recent years suggests that the influence may also work the other way round.

Exercise 4

It is widely believed that the internet is making our lives easier than they were in the past. (1) ~~Furthermore~~, the internet is used as a consultation method for solving many problems. (2) ~~On the one hand~~, many people use the internet for consulting others who are in a different location, for example, teachers, physicians and community researchers. (3) Moreover, there are social networking sites such as Facebook to communicate with old friends, and so you can get together with them and other people you have

not seen in a long time. The internet has (4) ~~also~~ led to an increase in opportunities for face-to-face communication and people can talk with each other at any time and anywhere. (5) ~~At last,~~ people with disabilities can use the internet to help overcome obstacles so that they have better access to education and other services.

1 **Furthermore:** the reader has just read a sentence that says what is widely believed (that the internet makes our lives easier). This linking word suggests that there is something else that is widely believed. Instead, the sentence gives an example of how it makes our lives easier.

2 **On the one hand:** this is always followed by 'on the other hand' (which is missing here), to give opposing points of view. There are no views expressed here: there are examples given here about how the internet can solve problems. This connects the sentence to the previous sentence, and a linking word was not absolutely necessary.

3 **Moreover:** this is acceptable as it introduces a second point. The first point was that it helps solve problems, the second that it helps with communication, and both points are evidence that the Internet is making our lives easier.

4 **also:** this suggests that there is another idea, but actually face-to-face communication was already mentioned in the previous sentence ('get together with them').

5 **At last:** this is incorrect. 'At last' is not used in academic writing. It suggests that it has taken too long. Instead, you can use 'last', 'lastly' or 'finally.'

The student seems to have used incorrect and unnecessary linking words to give the impression that the paragraph is developed well. Unfortunately, not only will the reader notice immediately that this is not the case, he or she will also be confused about what the student is trying to say.

Exercise 5

Internet users can get information any time <u>they</u> need it via <u>their</u> internet connection. When the internet was first introduced, <u>its</u> feature was to share information. As time has gone by, more functions and tools have been added. <u>These</u> include blogs, <u>which</u> allow users to share <u>their</u> comments and opinions, and social networks, <u>which</u> enable people to pass on messages quickly.

- 'they' and 'their' refer to internet users.

- 'its' refers to the internet.

- 'These' refers to functions and tools.

- 'which' refers to blogs.

- 'their' refers to users.

- 'which' refers to social networks.

The connections between the sentences indicated by pronouns all suggest that the writer is giving a list, which is related to the topic of the internet.

Chapter 3

Exercise 1
Suggested answers:

Comprehension is commonly defined as the act of understanding.

The act of understanding is known as comprehension.

Exercise 2
1 which / that	3 which / that
2 which / that, which / that	4 who
	5 which / that

Exercise 3
1 exemplifying	3 giving cause/effect
2 listing/classifying	4 comparing/contrasting

Exercise 4
1 a This essay **has discussed** the economic factors that contributed to ...

  b In this essay, I **have argued** that globalization is not a recent phenomenon.

  c This essay **has explored** the causes of the conflict ...

2 You could have used a simple past (e.g. *this essay discussed*). However, the present perfect, as in the answers above, is better because the essay is not finished yet.

3 a These findings **suggest** that ...

  b The evidence **seems** to indicate that ...

  c A consequence of this **is** that ...

If you are repeating exactly what you have already said, you could use the simple past (*These findings suggested that ...*). It is very common in conclusions to use the present simple when discussing the significance of findings and evidence.

Chapter 4

Exercise 1
The style in this book is informal. The informal style has been chosen because this book is giving advice directly to the readers. The pronouns 'we' and 'you' make the text more personal. A friendly style is appropriate because the text aims to be reassuring.

Here are some examples from this section of Chapter 4:

- *Try to work out what the mistakes are and how you could correct them before you read on.*

'Try to work out' is a command – the writer is addressing the reader. The use of 'you' makes the text more personal and direct.

- *Idioms are very rare in academic writing, and it is better if you don't use them.*

Contractions are not used in a formal style.

- *There is a grammatical mistake here: you wouldn't say 'every X cannot'.*

A more formal way of writing this would be 'it is wrong to say ...', but the use of 'you' makes the style less formal; the use of the contraction in 'wouldn't' is informal.

Exercise 2
Suggested answers:

1 Better staff training will increase the company's efficiency. / With better staff training the company's efficiency will increase.

2 In this case, cultural differences necessitate varied communication strategies.

3 The adoption of this strategy may lead to cost reductions.

4 The creation of such a unit may improve the accessibility of marketing information.

Exercise 3

Suggested answers:

1 Non-verbal behaviour has significant effects on every living **being.**

2 This environment is non-living **components** like rocks, water and air.

3 It is necessary from a social point of view to talk about unimportant **topics** sometimes.

4 Giving pupils more responsibilities during an already stressful time may not be the wisest **action to take.**

5 Stress may not be as negative a **factor** for our health as previously thought. / Stress may not be as negative for our health as previously thought. (i.e. simply take 'thing' out)

Exercise 4

Suggested answer:

> Schoolchildren may be able to improve their mathematical knowledge and skills with regular practice outside the classroom. This will help them avoid an over-reliance on calculators, although those can still be helpful when checking answers or doing long calculations.

Chapter 5

Exercise 1

1 Complex and currently unresolved <u>issues</u> arising in research on innovation in complex organizations **are** also to be examined.

2 Lastly, a possible <u>solution</u> of the horizon, flatness, homogeneity and isotropy problems in cosmology **is** suggested.

3 Hundreds of reliable focal-mechanism <u>solutions</u> for deep and intermediate depth earthquakes **were** analysed.

Exercise 2

To begin with, it is essential to understand what the feminist approach is, why it has emerged and what its positions are. According to Saratankos (2005:71) the feminist approach is defined as 'an established type of research, which has the specific purpose of studying women and their status in the community'. Put differently, women are the dominant research subject of the feminist approach, which aims at attaining economic, social and political equality between the sexes, emancipating women and increasing people's understanding about blatant sexism.

Chapter 6

Exercise 1

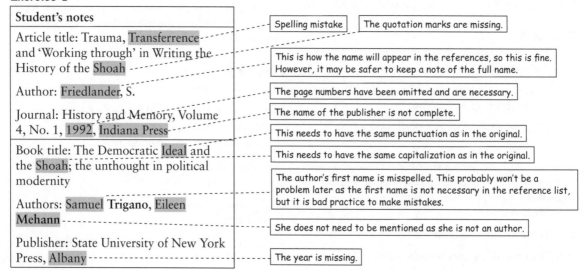

Student's notes	
Article title: Trauma, Transferrence and 'Working through' in Writing the History of the Shoah	Spelling mistake · The quotation marks are missing.
Author: Friedlander, S.	This is how the name will appear in the references, so this is fine. However, it may be safer to keep a note of the full name.
Journal: History and Memory, Volume 4, No. 1, 1992, Indiana Press	The page numbers have been omitted and are necessary. · The name of the publisher is not complete. · This needs to have the same punctuation as in the original.
Book title: The Democratic Ideal and the Shoah; the unthought in political modernity	This needs to have the same capitalization as in the original. · The author's first name is misspelled. This probably won't be a problem later as the first name is not necessary in the reference list, but it is bad practice to make mistakes.
Authors: Samuel Trigano, Eileen Mehann	She does not need to be mentioned as she is not an author.
Publisher: State University of New York Press, Albany	The year is missing.

Exercise 5

1 university / concert hall

2 post-traumatic stress / symptoms

3 knowledge management / systems

4 solid waste / management

5 data stream / systems

6 social science / issues

7 human resource / management

8 economic growth / theory

Chapter 8

Exercise 1

This essay is biased (1) because it does not consider the evidence against the writer's opinion. There are also examples of items 2, 4, 5, 6 and 9 in the essay.

> (2) Because of the spread of the world's economic crisis, more and more people are asking for a single world currency system. (6) Therefore, it is a good idea to implement this.
>
> First, the risks involved in foreign exchange would no longer exist if we had a single world currency. In international trade, enterprises (4) always face exchange rate risks. The loss caused by the floating exchange heavily counteracts their profit. Sometimes trading loss occurs in a very short time.
>
> Second, it would be very convenient if we had a single world currency: people would not need to exchange money or pay service charges in the future. (4) Everybody (2) wants convenience above everything else when they travel, (6) so one currency is better.
>
> Last but not least, the competitive power of enterprises would improve if the prices for the goods and service were in same currency. It would be beneficial to social development.
>
> Some say that it would be difficult to manage the currency, (5) but these are the usual (2) pessimistic economists. (9) Given the evidence in favour above, it is clear that a single world currency should be put into practice in the future.

Note: in the first example of 2 above, evidence is necessary because the statement which has been made is so strong.

Chapter 9

Exercise 1

1 and **2** are common knowledge and do not need a citation.

3 This could be common knowledge but is actually a dictionary definition (taken from the Cobuild online dictionary) so it needs a citation.

4 This is an interesting and concise way of expressing an opinion about history: that there may be different versions of history and that the official history is only one version of what really happened, but the most popular one. This particular statement has been attributed to Napoleon Bonaparte, so it needs a citation.

5 This is a more controversial statement than the previous one. It has been attributed to Ambrose Bierce and needs a citation.

Exercise 2

1, 2, 3, and **7** are well-known facts, although 1 and 7 perhaps only in certain disciplines.

4 This is the opposite of (3), which is considered a fact under normal circumstances, so it will either need explaining (under what circumstances is this true?) or you will need to cite the source before explaining further.

5 This definition is very specific ('any paid form of non-personal presentation') and sounds academic. It is different from the general definition of advertising which you would find in a dictionary. If you find a definition like this on a website and cannot determine the author, check that the site has not just taken it from elsewhere without saying so. It is up to you to determine its real origin, which actually is a book by Kotler and Armstrong (2001).

6 This is a controversial statement that would need explanation and/or a reference.

8 This is not well-known, and does not sound academic. If you really wanted to make this point, you would have to evidence it.

Exercise 3

Essay A

(1) *Cars have been debated for many years.
Some say that they are convenient, whereas
other people say that they are expensive, and
cause problems for traffic, human beings and the
environment. As they cause so many problems,
governments should ban cars.*

*Many people have cars because they are available
when and where they want them. If they want
to go and visit family in a different city, they can
just take their car and drive to the right address.
If they took a train, they would still need to
get to the station, and the train might not stop
close to the address they want. Trains and buses
do not travel at night, so they would not be
able to visit family at certain times. Businesses
also rely on road transport. Cars give people
convenience, so they don't usually mind that they
are expensive to buy and maintain (repairs and
petrol) because it is worth it for them.*

*However, (2) convenience is the only
advantage that cars offer, and there are many
disadvantages. Firstly, people die because of cars.
(3) More people die on the road than in other
types of accidents and many are children on
their way to school. (4) People also die in road
rage incidents when people get angry with other
drivers for driving badly. (5) They could also die
or suffer from the pollution that cars cause, e.g.
asthma is increasing.*

*Secondly, pollution causes damage to the
environment. Most cars still use petrol,
which causes damage. Moreover, building
cars and motorways is bad for the environment
too.*

*Lastly, these problems are going to increase
because there are too many cars already and
ownership will keep increasing. Having more
cars also means more traffic jams, which will
have a negative influence on business if they
make business people miss appointments.*

*In conclusion, the disadvantages outweigh the
advantages, so cars should be banned.*

1   In a more academic essay, you would provide
examples of 'debates' about cars, or details of a
source that mentions these.

2   This is a strong statement to make. It really needs
evidence, in the form of a source that has said
this. If this is the writer's own opinion and not
based on a source, and there is no other evidence
available to back this up, then it needs to be
rephrased more cautiously: 'most important'
instead of 'only' or 'is probably' instead of 'is'.

3   These statistics cannot be given without evidence.

4   There needs to be some sort of evidence, e.g. a
mention of newspaper reports about this.

5   There has to be a source for the fact that more
and more people suffer from asthma.

Exercise 4

1   This is a saying of unknown origin, but often
attributed to British Prime Minister Winston
Churchill. It can easily be paraphrased, but a
quote would be acceptable because the saying is
so short and to the point.

2   There is no good reason to quote, so this should
be paraphrased.

3   This is an often quoted sentence by Oscar
Wilde, a British playwright. He made a
very personal comment here which is quite
controversial, and he put it in a very interesting
way. This is something that would best be quoted.

Exercise 5

The student is trying to indicate that the
terminology is not her own, by putting words such
as 'explicit' between quotation marks. However,
as she has not mentioned whose words and
definitions (between brackets) these are, it is still
plagiarism.

Exercise 6

1   Correct.

2   Correct. As this was a quote, the page number
needed to be added.

3   Not correct: full stop needed after *et al*.

4   Correct.

5   Not correct: lower case a needed.

Exercise 7
The two additional sources are correct, but as the list should be alphabetical, Lapkin would come before Rivers.

Chapter 10

Exercise 1
Paraphrase 1
This paraphrase is making a claim that the original did not have: the first sentence is too general, making it sound as if it is about more than fashion. Also, the three countries were only given as examples of places with textile industries, rather than what is being said now, i.e. that the textile industry is an example of something bigger. The other factual mistake is that the West is influencing the East, as the original text claimed the opposite.

This paraphrase misrepresents the author, which is completely unacceptable.

Paraphrase 2
Although this paraphrase does not include every detail of the original text, remember that it does not need to: this was part of a larger text anyway, which will not be paraphrased completely. This paraphrase is the best one of the three: it reflects what the original author was saying but it has been used in a new (but related) argument with a slightly different emphasis: it is about familiarity rather than influence, and perhaps the writer will continue the topic of the textile industry.

Paraphrase 3
This paraphrase is too close to the original. Although the writer has not used many of the words from the original, he has used synonyms throughout (*fashion – clothing trends, influenced – affected, for many years – for a long time, Eastern culture – culture from the East*, etc.) and has not demonstrated any real understanding of the original, which means he has only demonstrated language skills, not academic skills. The pattern is also similar to the original (see e.g. the first sentence).

This can be considered plagiarism as using synonyms and changing word order is a technical exercise. This technique is more about hiding the original quote, rather than paraphrasing and integrating it well to show it has been understood and developed into a new argument.

Exercise 2
The second paraphrase is better because it develops the ideas of the writer better. The writer's first topic sentence talks about how the fashion industry has recently been influenced by Africa. The paraphrase functions as a second topic sentence, talking about the more long-term trend of Eastern influence. The phrase 'long-term trend' at the beginning of the paraphrase is linked, through contrast, to the word 'recently' in the first sentence of the text.

The first paraphrase also relates to what was said in the original text, but it is not integrated in the essay: 'also' does not really tell us much, so we do not know how the paraphrase supports the writer's ideas or develops them. The writer has not demonstrated an understanding of the original well enough.

Exercise 3
The essay

> Some scientists have suggested that dolphins are so intelligent that they should be treated as a person, albeit a non-human one. **They found some similarities between dolphins and humans in terms of the anatomy of their brains and what they can do with them, e.g. learning, teaching, communicating, and thinking about the future (Burns, 2010).** This raises questions about how dolphins are being treated now.

Notes about the six steps (FRANCIS):

Step 1 (F) Note that the information about chimpanzees was not selected because it did not fit. You should only select from your source what is useful for the development of your own ideas.

Step 4 (N) <u>dolphins similar to humans</u>: communication, smarter than three-year-old humans, anatomy of brain, think about future, learn and teach

Exercise 4
1 e 2 d 3 c 4 f 5 a 6 b

Exercise 5
1 f 2 b 3 e 4 d 5 a 6 c

Exercise 6

Presenting facts		Presenting opinion	
acknowledge	indicate	allege	claim
demonstrate	prove	argue	imply
point out		assert	propose
			suggest

Exercise 7

What is the writer's opinion? The implementation of anti-discrimination actions which have long-term effects is therefore forgotten when managers have to deal with other urgent issues.

Does the writer agree with the sources she quotes? Yes.

Do the sources express the same idea, or are they separate components of the argument? There are two different ideas here: ignoring equality actions (in small companies), and prioritizing profit (in all companies). Together they lead to the conclusion: the paragraph's last sentence.

Exercise 8

1 Redmond (2003: 12) defined the low income groups as 'Low income is defined as $725 or less'.

You would not repeat 'defined' and 'low income', but there is not much left in the quote without this – it may be better not to quote here.

2 According to Grelling (2006: 98), to protect the construction materials of the bridge they used 'Chemical additives used (...) in the concrete and waterproofing systems'.

After 'they used' you need the object, a noun phrase without a verb. If you remove a word from the original quote, you need to show that there is something missing by using (...).

3 Atkins (2010: 42) said **that** Burj Al Arab was 'the world's most luxurious and tallest all-suite hotel in Dubai'.

'that' introduces a sub-clause, which needs to have a verb. We could not add a verb to the original text, so needed to do this outside of the quotation marks.

Exercise 9

The authors ...

1 **concluded** that all languages have them.

2 **argued** that all languages have them.

3 **identified** that all languages have them. / **identified** them in all the languages in the sample.

4 **claimed** that all languages have them.

5 **implied** that all languages have them.

Note: it is not possible to use 'how all languages have them' in these sentences.

Exercise 10

1 a **reported** (what the researchers did is emphasized)

   b **indicated** (what the researchers did is emphasized)

2 **have revealed** (a number of studies, no named authors or dates in the subject)

3 a **showed** (this was true at that time)

   show is also possible as you could say that the data always show this

   b **were**: the information refers to patients that were a certain age at that time, so this verb needs to be in the past.

Chapter 11

Exercise 1

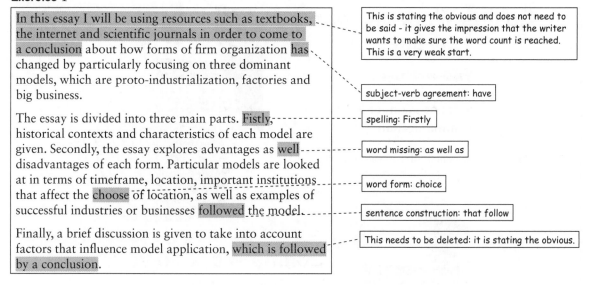

In this essay I will be using resources such as textbooks, the internet and scientific journals in order to come to a conclusion about how forms of firm organization has changed by particularly focusing on three dominant models, which are proto-industrialization, factories and big business.

> This is stating the obvious and does not need to be said - it gives the impression that the writer wants to make sure the word count is reached. This is a very weak start.

> subject-verb agreement: have

The essay is divided into three main parts. Fistly, historical contexts and characteristics of each model are given. Secondly, the essay explores advantages as well disadvantages of each form. Particular models are looked at in terms of timeframe, location, important institutions that affect the choose of location, as well as examples of successful industries or businesses followed the model.

> spelling: Firstly

> word missing: as well as

> word form: choice

> sentence construction: that follow

Finally, a brief discussion is given to take into account factors that influence model application, which is followed by a conclusion.

> This needs to be deleted: it is stating the obvious.

Exercise 2

1

Introduction	Methods	Results	Discussion and conclusion
■ relevance of the problem ■ the background of the problem/project ■ the purpose of the report/research ■ relevant research about the topic	■ design/procedure of survey/experiment ■ how the information was gathered / the experiment was carried out	■ outcome of the experiment/survey/comparison ...	■ summary of the project/research ■ suggestions for further reading ■ description of the meaning and significance of the findings, e.g. whether they were expected or not ■ limitation of methods, materials and other aspects

2 The main part is the Results section.

Exercise 3

1 The writer studies Electrical Engineering / Electronic Engineering. The text is part of a report about a design project. Her brief was to develop an electronic product, e.g. a game or mobile phone. This particular paragraph comes from the evaluation section. Notice the formality of the style.

2 The writer studies International Development/Business/Economics. This is a diary entry from the first term of his studies, in which students were encouraged to reflect on the differences and similarities with their previous studies (in other countries). The students were asked to particularly comment on different learning situations and formats, on working with others, on expectations and on learning experiences.

Notice the mixture of styles: in this piece of reflective writing the student writes in a personal way ('I thought ...) but still uses an academic style. In a personal diary he might have expressed his feelings about the two people in the group in a very different way (e.g. 'Samuel and Angela started to argue about something really stupid, we tried to stop them but they would not listen!!!').